SUCK IT UP, PRINCESS

PRAISE FOR *SUCK IT UP, PRINCESS*

"Natalie Sisson's new book will leave you inspired, motivated, and ready to take action to create the life you want. This is the no-nonsense, loving kick in the pants you've been waiting for. It's time to do more, and be more."

—DORIE CLARK, AUTHOR OF *REINVENTING YOU* AND EXECUTIVE EDUCATION FACULTY, DUKE UNIVERSITY FUQUA SCHOOL OF BUSINESS

"Natalie's book might just be the (gentle and loving) smackdown you need right now to shake yourself off and start again! Full of tips on how to get out of your own way, *Suck it Up, Princess* is the perfect antidote to imposter syndrome — so we can just get over our inner critic and get on with achieving our dreams."

—DENISE DUFFIELD-THOMAS, AUTHOR OF *CHILLPRENEUR* AND FOUNDER OF MONEY BOOTCAMP

"Natalie Sisson delivers what we all need when we are sabotaging our own success: a fun, fresh and honest kick in the pants. You will be inspired by her victories, learn from her mistakes and leave the book ready to slay your own dragons."

—PAMELA SLIM, AUTHOR, *BODY OF WORK*

"I think we're all craving more honest peeks behind-the-scenes of people who have created epic lives and businesses, and Natalie delivers. If you're ready to get out of your own way, and unleash the power and potential you know you hold within you, dive into this book!"

—NATALIE MACNEIL, EMMY AWARD-WINNING MEDIA ENTREPRENEUR + COACH TO LEADERS AND CHANGEMAKERS AT NATALIEMACNEIL.COM

"Look beyond the title — there are gems of wisdom inside! I'll be straight — as someone who values kindness, the phrase "suck it up, princess" isn't my jam. So I'd usually walk by a title like this - but as they say don't judge a book by its cover! Surprisingly compassionate, and definitely smart and real (much like Natalie), this is a beautiful read — especially if you're usually a go-getter (but have been going through a bit of a slump in an area of your life or work)."

—MARIANNE CANTWELL, TEDX SPEAKER (THE HIDDEN POWER OF NOT ALWAYS FITTING IN) AND AUTHOR OF *BE A FREE RANGE HUMAN*

"Put your Warrior Princess pants on! Natalie Sisson is bringing the tough love in *Suck It Up, Princess*. Her elegant authenticity is perfectly paired with actionable advice and will get you fast-tracked to going after the life you want!"

—AMY SCHMITTAUER LANDINO, AUTHOR OF *GOOD MORNING, GOOD LIFE* AND *VLOG LIKE A BOSS*, AND CREATOR OF THE AWARD-WINNING YOUTUBE SERIES AMYTV

"Natalie Sisson's latest book *Suck it up, Princess* is THE mindset book for ambitious women who want to make an impact but are keeping themselves stuck with perfectionism, imposter syndrome and the feeling that they are not enough. With personal stories, adventures, case studies and concrete steps Natalie shows the reader how she can start to live up to her full potential — as a princess or queen."

—SIGRUN GUDJONSDOTTIR, BUSINESS COACH, TEDX SPEAKER AND HOST OF THE SIGRUN SHOW

SUCK IT UP, PRINCESS

Real-life strategies to be the heroine you already are and have the money, success and life you deserve

NATALIE SISSON

Published by Tonawhai Press

www.nataliesisson.com

ISBN 978-0-473-56137-6 (softcover)
ISBN 978-0-473-56139-0 (hardcover)
ISBN 978-0-473-56141-3 (epub)
ISBN 978-0-473-56143-7 (PDF)
ISBN 978-0-473-56145-1 (audiobook)

To my Mum, Gina.

Your full name, Regina, embodies the Queen you truly are. Thanks for showing this Princess what true strength, determination, love, honesty, and elegance truly are.

CONTENTS

THIS BOOK IS FOR YOU

You have big things you want to put out in the world, lady!

You're here to make a dent. Create an impact. Leave a legacy.

But sometimes:

- Your inner critic derails your best-laid plans.

- Imposter syndrome plagues you like a shadow, stopping you in your tracks.

- And procrastination, that bitch, rears her ugly head, every time you get inspired and start creating.

Or are these all really just excuses? Do you need to Suck It Up, Princess, and develop the right mindset, habits, and strategies to kick ass and go for it in work and in life?

Suck It Up, Princess is an inspiring, refreshingly honest, witty, fun, loving, and ass-kicking book, designed to show you where you can take control of your life and bring out your inner heroine.

You'll learn, as I have, when you need to forge ahead and 'just do it' and when you need to slow down, and show yourself some damn compassion!

When the best times are for self-love, fine wine, and time with your best girlfriends.

When life-affirming mantras, incense, and a yoga mat could be just the breakthrough you're looking for.

And when you need to get out of your own way and give yourself permission to dream big, and 'do' bigger.

As someone who's always gone for it in every area of life—being a goal-getter, smashing world records, and getting a gold medal in Ultimate Frisbee—I felt I had a pretty good handle on what it takes to live an awesome life.

Add to that quitting the rat race in 2008 and buying a one-way plane ticket to Canada to start and build a multiple-six-figure blog and education business while living out of a suitcase and travelling the world full-time.

Life was fabulous and I thought I had it all together.

That was until I came back to my homeland of New Zealand and did a complete 180-degree change in my life and work, which took me two damn years to get over, and threw into the air all I knew in the world to be true.

What's more, it took some deep diving into myself, personal growth, massive amounts of reflection, some awesome failures that rattled me to my core, and a sucky period of...well, feeling sucky, for me to realise the truth:

> I did not have my shit together. I was not better than anyone. I was not special. I was not successful. I was just me, and that was more than enough. From there sprang deep-seated joy, knowing, learning, understanding, and happiness, combined with going right back to the basics.

I highly advise this process if you want to really get to know yourself at any stage of your life, especially in your early 40s, when what you think you know about yourself is just dangerous.

That's why this book burst out of me. Part memoir, part self-help guide, and part collection of random stories, it's broken down into short chapters that are highly digestible, easy to take in and take action on.

Think of it as your best friend and your handbag guide to busting out your inner Warrior Princess when you need her most.

I cover hot topics that you'll frankly be dealing with all your life, like getting over yourself, realising that you are not your ego, getting rid of imposter syndrome, the power of saying no, and valuing your gorgeous self, to name a few.

Unlike my previous books, this book is not filled with a plethora of tools, software, and case studies. It is, however, packed with love, my own stories, radical transparency, silliness, hard truths, and legit guidance, plus tips and proven methods to get out of your own way to be the heroine you know you already are.

My intention is that this will be a 'read it in a weekend but leave an imprint for a lifetime' type of book. Also known as your handbag bestie, because you can just whip this book out when you need a quick fix, helpful advice, or a truth bomb in the moment! This leaves you zero excuses not to dive into it right NOW, sister!

Suck It Up, Princess is for women the world over who are playing it small, or not playing at all, who are hiding their gifts from the world and need a girlfriend/sister/bestie/moach (mentor and coach) to show them how to start living as their best self.

It's for women in business, at the helm of their own ship, who have simply veered off course, or hit some rough seas (puking ain't fun) and need to reset their navigation to sail in the right direction again, with the help of their co-pilot (that's me, lovely).

It's for women who thought they had it all together, and have reached a stage in their life where they realise they don't at all and are wondering: What the fuck do I do now?

Or they've achieved their wildest dreams and are wondering what their new 'why' should be, and trying to figure out how they've gotten to this place after everything they've done.

And it's for women, like you and me, who simply love reading a great book that makes them laugh, cry, snort, resonate, ponder, reflect, take action, and become a heroine of their own life!

The title of this book has now become my new mantra, and I hope it becomes yours.

PART 1

UNLEASH YOUR INNER HEROINE

The dictionary definition of a heroine is:
a woman admired for her courage, outstanding
achievements, or noble qualities.

Part 1 is all about understanding your inner world, which,
let's face it, is the key to understanding pretty much
everything in life, and the only one you have the power to
change to be exactly who you desire to be.

MY SUCK IT UP, PRINCESS MOMENT

It was a rainy day in late January 2020 and I was in a funk. This was a deep funk that had been hanging around like a bad smell for almost a month, and I simply couldn't shake it. It left me feeling heavy, sad, and a little bit hopeless. I had no motivation to do anything of significance and I was always tired. And what's worse, it seemed to be for absolutely no reason.

Outwardly, life was grand. My partner, Josh, and I had just moved into this incredible property, our 'forever home', with 10 acres of land, a mix of field and trees, with a gentle gurgling river running through it. I'd just competed in and finished my first ever half Ironman—or Ironwoman, as I prefer to call it—after over a year of training for triathlons and building up my mental and physical prowess.

To top it off, I'd finally fallen back in love with my business and got my 'launching' mojo back, with a new offering I shared with my community in November, aptly named 'Launch Your Damn Course'. Not only did I feel in flow again, designing, launching, and running it live, but it also sold out not one, but two cohorts, in quick succession!

So why was it, then, that I found myself standing in our lovely local park on a drizzly Tuesday afternoon, while out walking my two gorgeous dogs, with tears streaming down my face? I had done my gratitudes that morning and had everything to be happy about in life, and yet here I was. Sad as fuck. With no apparent reason at all.

Now I'm all for a bit of wallowing when you need it. I'm all for showing yourself compassion and nurturing your need to just 'feel' into your emotions. But this was different. And in that very moment, tired of feeling tired, sad, pitiful, a voice spoke from the depths of my soul:

'Oh just SUCK IT UP, PRINCESS!'

I was so taken aback at saying those words out loud that for a split second I was shocked. Shocked that I was telling myself off, and doing it in style! Shocked that it had felt like an inner voice that was definitely mine but not within my control, that had just handed me a cold hard slap of reality I so desperately needed.

The result? I promptly burst out laughing. I laughed so hard I cried, but they were tears of joy and relief, like I'd finally gotten the punch line at a comedy show. I felt instantly lighter, and I realised in that moment I had just sucked it up, like a princess, and snapped myself out of a ridiculous, long-lasting relationship with Mr Doldrums.

Damn, it felt good.

Sharing this story later that day, my friend burst out laughing and said, 'That should be the name of your next book'. And so here we are: a phrase blurted out in pure desperation at a version of Natalie, who realised she simply needed to suck it up, Princess.

> *The Urban Dictionary* defines 'Suck It Up, Princess' as:
>
> 1. Do things with less whining
>
> 2. Quit whining.

It's slightly more appropriate and less offensive than a common saying used by my Australian friends and me over the years: 'harden the fuck up'. But it has the same effect, and it's a powerful coaching tool to use on yourself. That voice of 'suck it up' is crucial, especially when we're giving our emotions too much credit.

There's a time for empathy and compassion, and there's also a time when we get too soft and overwhelmed with how everything *should* be and when it's not, we turn it into a big deal and act like a drama Queen.

And instead of calling yourself out on this, there's a big honouring of various excuses:

- 'Oh, that must have hurt when your mom did that.'

- 'My goodness, was it tough on Tuesday?'

- 'That sounds so difficult. Tell me more'.

It's in these moments where we can say to ourselves: Hey, Suck It Up, Princess. Suck It Up, Buttercup. Let's move on. This snaps you out of your story that you've become very attached to, and instead gets you to focus on putting one foot in front of the other and to keep walking.

It's a huge superpower to have. It says, 'Let's not take your upset too seriously, because other bad stuff can happen too that's *actually* more important. Like a pandemic sweeping the world—that puts everything into perspective, right?'

When all else fails, when you hear yourself making excuses, getting down on yourself, having a pity party, letting your inner critic take over, with no respite, simply take a deep breath, and say, or yell out loud:

'Oh Suck It Up, Princess!'

Then get on with what you were *really* wanting to do in the first place.

You're welcome!

FEEL THE FEAR AND DO IT ANYWAY

Who the heck flies to Nairobi, Kenya, and attempts to cycle 6,500km (4,000 miles) through seven countries, and finish up in Cape Town, South Africa? Well me, and if my memory serves me correctly, about 50 other crazy people who biked even further.

Each and every one of us was called to this adventure from Tour d'Afrique in 2012, for completely different reasons. Some were lost and wanting to find themselves. Others had quit their jobs and were taking a year off. A few had ended a long relationship or marriage and simply had to get away. Several were cycling enthusiasts and were there to race from Cairo to Cape Town.

Me? I was looking to get out of my comfort zone and live on the edge, because that's where growth happens. I knew this trip would be challenging. I didn't know it would be epic, redefining, and life changing.

It's also the only time I've personally had a sore butt for 60 days in a row. It never stopped hurting! This bike ride turned out to be a huge test of whether I could get through cycling huge distances every day—not only physically but mentally—and also whether my online business could survive me abandoning it for two whole months!

Along with training for this ride (poorly), and preparing my business for it (hiring a virtual assistant two weeks before leaving), I decided to add to the challenge further, by raising money for an awesome charity.

Why would a sane person do this to themselves? I've asked myself that question quite a lot, at other times in my life too.

Because, why the hell not?!

The reason I do things that take me out of my comfort zone is I know from experience that doing so only makes you stronger, braver, and more resilient. The sweet spot is right on the edge of your comfort zone, where you can learn to appreciate the tingly mix of fear and excitement and dance on the edge. This allows you to be bold, yet stay safe at the same time. It's the place of expansion.

As you can well imagine, there were many Suck It Up, Princess, moments in this adventure. I thought I'd share a few of my favourites, just in case you find yourself doing something as crazy, or crazier, in your lifetime.

Some background context to set the scene. I've done a series of cool things every four years or so since 2004, including training for and winning a body sculpting competition, dragon boating across the English Channel to smash a world record, and winning a gold medal in Beach Ultimate Frisbee with Great Britain's women's team in Brazil.

So when 2012 rolled around, I felt it was time for my next adventure. I'd never done anything other than commuter cycling up until this point, so I knew this would be a huge challenge and a great way to visit a continent that's been on my list of places to travel to since I was a kid.

I also used it as a reason to support something much bigger than just my own personal goal. I wanted to raise money for a charity perfectly aligned with my values in life: **Women Win**, which empowers young girls in developing countries through sport. With the help of 190 contributions from my friends, family, peers, and community, I somehow managed to surpass my ambitious US$10K fundraising goal, and gave US$12,612 to Women Win.

In fact, the fundraising alone for this charity was like having a full-time job. I often felt overwhelmed with what I'd taken on, well before the ride even started. I'm not sure I fully advise biting off *that* much, but deep down, I knew this ride would be so much more meaningful if it wasn't just the ride of my own life, but riding for the life of others.

Was I scared? Oh heck yeah. I knew this would push me way out of my comfort zone. Nothing can prepare you for biking an average of 100km (60 miles) or more per day. I didn't even purchase the bike I rode on until the first week of February, one month before I started Tour d'Afrique.

I started training in the hilly suburbs of my hometown of Wellington, when I was back visiting New Zealand. If you know Wellington, you know how hilly, windy, and cold it can get—not always pleasant riding conditions. I competed in a 48km race, a 100km race, and then the Lake Taupo Cycle Challenge of 160km to show myself that I could survive that distance.

I was quite psyched up for the challenge of doing a similar distance day in, day out for two months, but I'm not sure I was fully prepared for the challenge mentally—it's something that you just need to experience for yourself.

There was an array of unexpected challenges. Aside from just cycling 6,500km over two months, I also had to contend with the routine of each day:

- Getting up at 5 a.m., packing up all your camping gear

- Putting on your bike gear (again) and prepping for the day ahead

- Getting in line for food (you don't want to miss out on breakfast)

- Understanding the directions and route for the day ahead to avoid getting lost

- Completing the ride before sunset (otherwise the crew would pick you up in the truck)

- Unpacking your tent again after a long day of riding, and an outdoor shower

- Having dinner with everyone else and sharing your adventures of the day, or just taking some quiet time away from it all

- Getting some quality sleep—not as easy it might seem (incessant barking dogs, laughing hyenas, deafening crickets, locals partying).

In addition, there were the ongoing cultural changes of riding through seven different countries, with different languages and types of people, as well as varying climate (from hot and humid in Tanzania, to chilly when we reached South Africa). Plus, cycling with a group of around 50 people from all over the world was a big social experiment in itself, although it came to be loved by everyone at the end of it (well, almost everyone).

Aside from the terrain and the daily distances were other challenges like being run off the road by crazy buses or trucks on busy highways, or having bike problems like flat tyres. I had such a bad run of this particular problem at one point that I would wake up to see flat tyres on my bike and want to cry. It's just the crappiest start to a new day and it sets you back, not only because of extra time but because it mentally saps your energy.

I just had to suck it up, Princess, and get over myself, because ain't no one gonna be empathetic to that shit, day in and day out, on a bike trip. I'm not implying that my fellow riders and the two mechanics weren't helpful, but everyone was there dealing with their own journey, and I realised this was my challenge to overcome. To this day, I'm fond of the nickname I earned during that period, Flatalie, which I was given after having a whole week of at least one flat tyre a day! Back then I could change a flat tyre in 60 seconds—I got that good at it!

The very first day of the ride taught me a lesson that's stuck with me for life: We are much more capable than we think. The only real limits you have are those you place on yourself.

How do I know this? Because I survived my first day on this journey, a mere 161km! It was hot, it was long (around 9 hours out on the road—including rests), and there was a horrific 30km off-road section of extreme corrugation (think sand, rock, and bone-jangling terrain).

I had to get off my bike and walk for five minutes when I noticed I was losing energy and struggling to breathe. Turns out it was a combination of heat stroke, the effect of my Malaria medicine in the sun, and lack of food! When I collapsed in my tent that night, I seriously wondered what I'd gotten myself into and how I was going to make it for the next two months.

But I did. Throughout the journey, there were hills that seemed never ending, sandy and rocky sections where we could barely hold on to the handlebars, and weather conditions that tested our endurance.

Our bodies may be able to endure just about anything; often it's our mindset and self-belief that need more work. The ability to just keep pedalling was something that never ceased to amaze me, even when I was struggling to find the mental energy and determination.

I share this genuinely life-changing experience to encourage you to regularly do something that scares the bejesus out of you. Perhaps that means doing a Facebook Live, speaking in front of a live audience, or having an honest conversation with an ex-partner.

Why? It's here you learn that it's not that scary after all, and you have *everything* within you to do what you're scared of, and go beyond to the next level of growth within you. If you want to push your boundaries but feel that fear is crippling you or holding you back, know that fear is a chemically induced state to help us proceed with caution, the fight-or-flight response. Without it, we would make dumb, impulsive choices.

Many times fear is a learned response. You might have grown up with parents who were nervous drivers. As a result, subconsciously you have always thought that driving should be met with extreme caution. And perhaps that's served you well in some instances. Fear is often an ally, but our bodies aren't perfect and there may be *irrational* fear holding us back.

Here's a test to measure if your fear is helpful and whether it should be embraced or ignored.

1. Create a list of pros and cons for a particular decision and score each one through ten for how relevant the reason is. Use this as a rational weighing scale to make your choice.

2. Next, take a deep breath, maybe even do a short meditation, and then ask yourself, 'Am I making this choice for me or for other people?' The aim here is to get rid of others' expectations of you.

3. Ask yourself better questions. If we want to find better answers, positive questions can reduce the amount of fear we feel and create a more accurate perspective from which to judge our choices.

4. Talk to friends who have been through a similar situation. They will understand and be able to guide you from a place of experience.

5. Explore the absolute worst-case scenario. What would happen if your worst fear came to light? Ask yourself if you could live with it. What you'll find is things won't be half as scary as you first thought them to be.

6. Forgive yourself. We're all on this journey together and none of us is perfect. Give yourself permission to make mistakes and good things will happen. Jim Carrey said this of playing life safe and not taking risks: 'You can fail at what you don't want, so you might as well take a chance on doing what you love'.

Don't forget, changing your mindset and doing things on the edge of your comfort zone, things that scare you, takes consistent action and practice. The benefits outweigh all the perceived fear, and the growth that ensues will feel liberating, even addictive.

Your new mantra is 'Feel the fear and do it anyway!'

IMPOSTER BE GONE

Were you having a productive day, and took a quick break to check your Instagram feed, only to find yourself still scrolling through 'perfect' photos 30 minutes later, and feeling like a loser?

Did you have a great idea for a business one morning, and by the afternoon you'd dug yourself into the hole of 'You're not good enough. How do you even think you could do this?'

Or maybe you were about to hit live on a course you've been working hard on for months, when you see a Facebook ad and realise that some lady has the exact same course topic and hers looks way better than yours. Deflated, you decide to just drop the whole thing.

Sound familiar? Despite excelling in your own field of expertise or knowing that you're truly capable, you still find that you're consciously comparing yourself to others, being paralyzed by that fear of not being good enough, feeling unworthy, or simply not being expert enough. You may even feel like a sham, someone who doesn't deserve to be on that stage or worthy of that recognition.

Enter *imposter syndrome.*

In my head he's a silhouette, with a cape and pointy hat, and sneaky slipper-type shoes. You don't see him coming, but you know when he's paid a visit. He enters your innermost precious thoughts, hopes, and dreams, just as you're getting ready to bring them to life, and suavely talks you out of them, and even attempts to derail you from your best-laid plans.

I've seen the effects he has on my incredible smart, talented, and capable clients and friends—it's devastating. He talks them out of taking action, showing up, thinking bigger, or just doing the thing they've always wanted to do.

He showed up in my mind too, right around the time I wanted to expand on my vision to go beyond what I'd done before, build a million-dollar business, speak on big stages, even put out this book. That's when he made his grand entrance, and despite my best intentions, I'd listen to him and worse, believe him.

I decided to dive deeper into this topic, because it turns out it's not a health risk or a disease, despite having the word 'syndrome' associated with it. But it damn well acts like one, when every person I speak to brings it up as the reason they are holding back.

I'm also happy to report that the antidote to imposter syndrome is this:

Suck It Up, Princess!

Yep, a healthy dose of that phrase can cure imposter syndrome in an instant. But it's unlikely to go away forever, because imposter syndrome is simply the awareness that you have a desire for something, but you don't think that you're enough to receive it.

The imposter phenomenon was first described by psychologists Suzanne Imes, PhD, and Pauline Rose Clance, PhD, in the 1970s. It typically occurs among us high achievers who are unable to internalise and accept our success. You have an awareness of what you desire, but you have a belief that contradicts it. And that leaves you feeling like you're a fraud. You feel like you're gonna be found out any day now, and that all your achievements to date were down to luck, rather than your awesome ability.

Psychologists agree that it is a very real and specific form of intellectual self-doubt. Impostor feelings are generally accompanied by anxiety and, often, depression.

Impostor syndrome and perfectionism often go hand in hand. So-called impostors think every task they tackle has to be done perfectly, and they rarely ask for help, which leads to two types of responses. You procrastinate, putting off doing the thing you really need to, out of fear that you won't be able to complete it to your impossibly high standards, or you overprepare and get stuck in the detail, researching, tweaking for eternity.

Either way—you still don't get it done!

Imposter syndrome is especially prevalent when you're embarking on a new endeavour, which is why those of us who are entrepreneurs get this so often, because this is the very nature of what we do. Every time you're on the edge of growth or a breakthrough, the imposter turns up to sabotage your dreams.

Well, I call BULLSHIT.

If you don't start giving yourself some credit, you'll ruin your chances of tapping into your full potential and going all in to achieve your dreams. Imposter syndrome is a limiting belief that can creep into the most important moments in your life, and turn them into a disaster. Here's how to overcome it.

Become self-aware.

Introspection is the first step to becoming self-aware. Being honest and understanding where and why it is impacting you are the first issues you should address. Is it because you feel that you lack the experience, knowledge, or skill set? If yes, then what have you done to act on it so you can cross that gap? Only when you get a sense of where you're currently at now can you determine how to realise your potential more fully and map out how to go to where you want to be.

Practice.

Once you've realised that these thoughts that keep bugging you and stopping you from being your best self are not permanent, then it's time to do the work. You need to put in the effort if you want to become better. If you believe that you are not there yet and you know where to improve, then practice, practice, and practice.

These days there are online courses for just about every topic area, at affordable prices. So if you feel that you need more mastery on a particular subject, sign up and learn. Continuously learning and applying it every day is practice in itself, but don't be too hard on yourself if you don't get it right away. Sometimes it takes years before you can master the ropes and get things right, and that's okay. You learn as you go.

Do it one task at a time.

Success doesn't come in one big package. It's the accumulation of all the small tasks that you do extremely well. In business, no one ever just hit the jackpot in one strike and remained there forever. In the same way, we can't assume we have the confidence before we have the skills.

Success is a consistent habit of persistently doing the small things the right way to achieve bigger goals, so do it one task at a time. Even having a checklist of your get-to-do's every day will not only help you feel more productive, but it will also help you get things done.

Avoid overthinking.

Usually, it's the overthinking that kills the dream even before you get started. Overthinking discourages you from even trying, so my advice is to focus on the tasks at hand. Direct your mind to what needs to be done.

Sometimes, we get a feeling that people are watching our every move, waiting for us to fail, but in reality we are all preoccupied, worrying about our own shit, and we don't have time to worry about anyone else.

So, the next time you're about to give a presentation or deliver a speech on stage, try not to overthink it, because more often than not, those people are probably more concerned about what they're going to do after the event, on the weekend, or what they're going to have for lunch.

Look forward so you can move forward.

Finally, look forward so you can move forward. The process doesn't have to be perfect, but you have to keep going. No one stays in one place; either you're expanding or you're shrinking. I vote for expansiveness every time!

Made a mistake? Learn from it and move on, because the moment you let your imposter feelings take over your actions is the moment you stop growing. Sometimes, you have to cut yourself some slack too, and take a moment just to breathe. A few hiccups aren't going to decide your future, but you have to keep going so you can keep on growing.

If you're at this point right now, it doesn't mean anything's wrong with you; it just means you're doing big important things that are out of your comfort zone. Not being where you want to be right now doesn't mean you won't get there in the future. And if it scares you, then all the more reason to take the plunge and flip that switch, Princess!

Remember: Imposter syndrome is self-centered and self-indulgent. If you believe strongly in what you do and its potential to impact others, and then you allow Mr Imposter to derail you and go unchecked, that's the most self-indulgent thing you can do, and it serves NOBODY.

Don't hold yourself to an impossible standard. Done is better than perfect. We don't need to be our best selves right now. We need the willingness to become them.

Imagine: who you can be without imposter syndrome? Damn magnificent, that's who!

NOTHING COMPARES TO YOU

It was a beautiful sunny morning as I stood on the edge of Lake Taupo, New Zealand, in the township of Kinloch, ready to start my first ever National Sprint Triathlon championship.

I'd spent three months preparing for this event, and now here I was in February 2019, wondering if I was actually ready for this triathlon, let alone the quest I'd started on to do my first Half Ironman race in December of that same year.

Triathlons (swim, bike, run) are one of the fastest-growing multi-sports in the world, and guess who's leading the charge? Yep, women like me between the age of 35 and 49, who are taking to it in droves.

Now, you might be wondering why the heck would someone want to swim in a cold lake or an ocean, follow that with a cycle ride that turns your legs to jelly, and then transition into a run that uses your muscles in a completely different way again, just so that you can cross the finish line and celebrate your own personal torture?!

I can let you in on a little secret. It's this little thing called a personal challenge, and triathlons happen to be one of the most challenging multidisciplined sports out there.

You see, what I've learned throughout my life and through my love of pursuing adventure and various sporting endeavours is that by pushing your boundaries, you reap great rewards in the form of personal and physical growth, like none other I've ever experienced in life.

There is massive reward from knowing that you trained for something, you turned up, you committed, and you crossed that finish line. It's an amazing sense of 'wow, I am capable'.

TRIATHLONS ARE A PERSONAL GROWTH JUNKIE'S TRIFECTA.

For me, I unlocked some more of my potential on this sunny day in February. I stretched myself in new ways. I dug deep within and I brought out my best.

What's best is that I was there doing it with all these other crazy, wonderful people who were on their own personal journeys, from professional athletes to inspirational

80-year-olds. Every single person was there for a different reason, and also because they'd all fallen in love with this sport called triathlon.

If you are already an experienced athlete, you may think that a 750m swim, followed by a 20km bike ride (in this case a very hilly ride), and then a 5km run is no sweat. You could get up tomorrow morning and do that, right?

I certainly couldn't. I hadn't been swimming in a long time, and even though I'm quite a capable swimmer, I found out that I'm not actually very fast. I have a good technique, but there's just so much that I can improve on, and swimming in a pool is completely different to swimming in an ocean with waves and saltwater, or in a lake with lots of people kicking and smacking you and, in my case, swimming right over me.

I've always had a love-hate relationship with running. In this particular year, I was determined to turn that into a full-blown love affair. I knew there was a tipping point, and when surpassed it that would give me the freedom I knew a love of running provides.

I took that on as my new mantra. (I hadn't yet started telling myself to Suck It Up, Princess.) That was my new reframe, and as a result I really look forward to running now and I've gotten better and faster at it, compared to when I did my first Splash and Dash race, a short swim in the ocean and then a run. I mean, you should have seen the photos of me. They weren't a pretty sight. I was so exhausted after a short 500m swim and 4km run, it seems embarrassing to remember it now.

Now, here I was, at this race three months later, feeling a lot fitter and stronger and starting to tap into my body's potential. I really thought I was going to do pretty well. I didn't have any grandiose ideas I was going to win, but I thought I could be pretty good at this sport, because I've always enjoyed a natural ability to play most sports well.

The joy and beauty of this sport of triathlon is that it's constantly messing with your mind and pushing you in ways that you didn't know were possible. Every time you turn up to a training or a race, there's going to be stuff going on in your mind:

- Stories you're telling yourself that you have to overcome

- Mental and physical limits you get to push through

- False messages about what you're capable of that you have to ignore

- And a new narrative that you can create.

We arrived early and got the opportunity to watch some of the elite triathletes doing time trials. I was amazed at how quick these athletes were, and many of them had been racing since they were seven years old.

Ok, no pressure, I thought. I'm not an elite triathlete, so I shouldn't even begin to compare myself with them. So I lined up with all the women in my age group, on the lake shores, and the horn went off. We all ran forward, and half tripped, half dived into the water.

It was brutal. I got swum over twice in the first 100m and was completely gobsmacked, as well as smacked in the head! (Looking at footage afterward that Josh shot, it was me who swam over someone while swimming on a diagonal!) I had to turn on my back briefly to suck in big gulps of air and compose myself. I honestly wanted to throw a tantrum or give up in that moment, but then I realised I was being a total Princess, so I carried on, and settled in to enjoy the beautiful clear and cold lake water.

I was one of the last women out of the water.

Thankfully, the bike ride was fantastic, with never-ending undulating hills. I managed to overtake some people going up, and I love whizzing downhill, so I was able to surpass the more cautious people.

Then it was on to the run, and by the time I started it was already hot and sunny. I didn't have a lot of transition experience from the bike to the run, or a heap of gas in the tank. I felt as if I was running like a tortoise. It was two laps of the same course, but even when you know what you're in for the second time around, that doesn't make it easier. Especially when most people have already finished, and there aren't many people left cheering, just the friendly volunteers saying, 'Keep it up, just two kilometers to go, you're almost there'.

Finally I got to run down the finishing chute and do a cartwheel (my 'famous' signature move to finish off any race) and got hugs and high fives from my friends who'd competed too.

Overall I was really happy that I competed in and completed this event, because it made the previous three months of training worthwhile. Yet when I found out I came in the bottom quarter in my race, division, and age group I was pretty disappointed. Suddenly I thought it sucked and told myself I'm not very good at this at all.

I remember standing there feeling deflated, when Josh reminded me, 'Nat, your goal was to finish and your goal was to get a certain time and you hit that and yet you're not happy'.

I responded, 'No, it's because I came in the bottom quarter of the whole field, which means I suck'.

He said, 'No, you set your intentions way too high. You've only been training for three months. This was the Nationals. This wasn't just some local event. This was the best of the best people turning up who were trying to qualify for World Champs and you made it to the end! You did well and you completed it and you should be happy with that. This is the first of many events'.

I'm glad Josh gave me a pep talk in that moment, and he had a fair point. Here I was out on this day comparing my beginner self with the rest of the field, who had years of experience of competing. My ego was showing up big time (more on how to overcome that in the next chapter).

I ended up speaking to a bunch of people after the race who had been doing triathlons for anywhere from two to ten years. One woman was 77; she had just won her age group and was off to the World Champs. It was amazing. And she said, 'I just love the sport. But it took me so long to get good at it and every single year it's just a small improvement that I make'.

'How long have you been doing them?' I asked.

'Oh, I've been competing for fifteen years'.

That put it in perspective for me. Right, play the long game, Nat!

Every single person I spoke to had the same energy. They said things like 'You can't just get good at a triathlon quickly', or 'There are very few people who are naturally good at it'. It's one of those things you just keep at it and you make improvements and continual upgrades to your training, to your nutrition, to your attitude. And it will come.

I'm pleased to say that since that race I moved up to come halfway through the field in events that I did. More recently I ran a 10km race in Wellington with thousands of people competing in it, and I was in the top third of the entire race group, for my gender and for my age group!

I was just thrilled because that proved to me that I had made massive strides in my running over a four-month period. And I always found the discipline of running to be my weakest—unless I'm running after a Frisbee or a ball. But I put my head down. I trained better. I believed in myself. I called myself a runner. I called myself an athlete. I trained with more focus and moved up from the bottom quarter to the top third.

It is all about the micro-improvements day after day, week after week. It was playing the long game and focusing on the journey, as much as on the results. It's about showing up, committing to consistent training, training with intention, and just continuing to get better, and most importantly, always enjoying it. Once I reframed, once I focused on being my best self and having the mindset of an athlete, everything changed.

My lesson here for you is that it's all about mind over matter. You have to have self-belief and then you have to put in the work to make it happen. The beauty is, this applies to any area in your life. The biggest takeaway is never to compare yourself to anybody else. You simply don't know where they started, or what it's taken for them to get to where you want to be.

As Sinead O'Connor wisely said, nothing compares to you.

BE MEANING*LESS*

I admit it. I am a meaning-making-machine. I'm also a ventriloquist for my dog.

Let me explain. I'll look at our beautiful white German shepherds Kayla and Angel, and they'll give me a look, or a sigh, or some body movement, and I immediately think I know what they're thinking.

'Ohhhh, she's looking at me with those eyes again. I think that means she really wants a gourmet dog bone and is bummed we haven't taken her on a walk yet'.

Josh usually laughs out loud at that point, and says, 'You can't possibly know what they're thinking, babe. You project on them so much and make their every look or move mean something'.

He has a point. It's a habit I'm getting better at kicking.

These are some variations of things I've made meaning out of before too. Any of them sound familiar to you?

- 'That lady just looked at me weirdly, did I offend her somehow?'

- 'Oh look, a rainbow, that's definitely a sign that we should buy this house'.

- 'Those three people didn't join my program. I guess that means they think it's shit'.

- 'That's the third time I've heard that today. Perhaps that means I'm on the wrong track?'

- 'That person didn't reply to my email. That must mean they're not interested in my proposal'.

- 'They didn't say anything about my new dress. Guess they don't think it suits me'.

- 'She's late to our lunch. Why doesn't she value my time?'

I mean, get a grip, lovely. Every single one of those thoughts going through your head was just that—a thought, not a fact. A made-up story that helps you make sense of the moment, not a truth, not an actual reality. Just your thoughts.

My thoughts had me attaching meaning to *everything*. Making up a story to fit what I saw, heard, and experienced through my own lens. I'm pretty certain you can relate.

Sometimes the meaning I was making was positive, but most of the time it was completely unrelated to the actual truth—and that can get you in trouble. In fact it's dangerous.

You see, your mind starts to recycle and replay these thoughts and then they become stories. The more you do this, the more you start to buy into it. These thoughts then become 'facts' in our mind and shape our behaviour and decisions.

You might think that's a good thing. Except that most of the time the stories we tell ourselves are hurtful, limiting, or damaging. The thing is, if you want to live life on your terms, the way you want, and feel and act the way you want to, you need to change the meaning making machine in your head.

So how do we do that? Various experts over the years have their methods, and most of them distill down to these steps:

1. Become aware of your thoughts.

2. Notice, observe, and challenge your thoughts.

3. Replace your thoughts with helpful ones that serve you.

Sounds so simple, and it actually freaking is!

I took you through an extended example of this in the previous section about getting over yourself, if you want to reread it.

Sure it takes effort to catch yourself in the moment and become aware that there's a thought going around in your head that isn't helpful. But if you don't interrupt your mind beavering away, you run the risk of believing those limiting thoughts, and letting them continue to tell you what's 'true'.

Next, you need to observe this thought and challenge or question if it's true. (Hint: it's unlikely to be.) The thought might be one you've told yourself for way too long—'I'm not good at [insert pretty much anything here: singing, dancing, writing, cooking, sex]'—so it might be harder to catch it. But once you have, you can determine whether it's hurting or helping you. If it's the former, then you get to learn to replace the negative thoughts with positive ones.

The thing is, when we change the way we think, we begin to change the way we feel. When you change the way you feel, and you start to *feel* different, guess what? You start to *behave* differently.

That's where the magic happens.

We act the way *we* want, and people sit up and take notice. They react to us in this new way we're being, and we start being our true selves, the ones with limitless potential. I know this to be true, because I've been doing the inner work, I've been working on becoming meaningless and it's incredibly freeing.

Give it a shot. You'll surprise yourself with how awesome it feels.

BEFRIEND YOUR INNER CRITIC

Do you have those annoying little voices inside your mind like I do? The inner critics that are just there to tell you why you're not good enough, expert enough, smart enough, just not enough. They're always there. They're always talking away at you, telling you why you're not going to be able to achieve something, why you shouldn't start something. But you can learn how to use your inner critics as a force for good.

Inner critics are brutal. They are harsh. They are loud or they whisper. They demand a lot and they're always there, telling you what you can and mainly what you can't do. But here's the thing—our inner critics are attempting to protect us, trying to keep us safe by not letting our imagination go wild with all the little things we can do and just saying, 'Hold back a little bit there, lady'.

In fact, I consider my inner critic a reflection of the very thing that I'm not showing up to do! So the inner critic is the truth of what I'm capable of. It's not actually there to keep me safe, to protect me. It's saying, 'Hey Natalie, look in the mirror. This is where you aren't showing up in the world. This is what you're fully capable of and you need to go and do that'.

Now that may sound really strange because typically we think inner critics are simply criticising us, but in this moment I realise that what that voice is doing is alerting me to what I can accomplish. The inner critics only show up for something that you deeply care about. That you're passionate about. That you really, really want to do. So if they appear when you're thinking about committing to doing *that* thing, that's a freaking great sign that you are on the right track.

For you, the inner critic might be your mother's voice, a bully from the past, or perhaps a physical shape or figure that appears in your mind. It might become triggered when you're on social media. In my case, this happens when I see fellow authors shouting out about their *New York Times* bestselling book on Instagram, or triathletes sharing their victory photos, or course creators squealing in delight at their sell-out launch. Or it might happen at networking events or at festivals. You may hear all sorts of inner critics at big gatherings—for example, *I don't dance like that person. I'm not dressed the right way. I'm not nearly as hip and cool as that person over there running naked through Burning Man* (a huge festival in the Nevada desert), and the list goes on.

But here's something meta to think about. Have you ever considered that your inner critic might actually have its own inner critics? I think my inner critic's biggest fear is me ignoring it and proving it wrong. It was in fact my four-year-old self, who's scared, and wants to be loved, and be a good person.

Our inner critic was born in our childhood and designed to keep us out of trouble and to prevent us from making mistakes over and over again. It remembers that mistake we made at a young age, plays that movie over and over and over again until we start to think that we're defective, that there's something wrong with us. But we don't realise that what we're hearing is just the same negative criticism playing in a loop. And no one can thrive under this attacking pattern.

So we need to face our inner critic to take away its power, to look it in the eye and say, 'This does not mean anything to me'. We need to understand that the inner critic is not steeped in truth and it is not part of realistic thinking. You can simply say, 'Hey, little version of me, it's okay. It's gonna be totally fine. Don't worry about it. I got this. You just stand back and watch me go. Hear me roar, "We're doing it!"'

It's important to remember that not all of your inner critics are there to take you down. Some of them may serve a positive purpose and hold some real wisdom for you. If you're a risk-taker, for example, who charges ahead without thinking about others or about the consequences, that inner critic may be the voice of reason for you. In many cases you just have to put that inner critic to one side and maybe bring it out a little later when you really need to hear it.

To truly understand how to quiet our inner critic, we need to understand where it lives in our brain because it is actually a very important part of how the mind works. The chemical that triggers the inner critic to start talking in your head is tied to the brain's threat protection system. This adrenaline-fueled arrangement is part of the fight-or-flight response to keep us safe and to enable us to learn from our mistakes.

But here's the problem. Sometimes it can go awry and start taking over everywhere. Studies have found that the inner critic may be triggered when there is no external threat; it's just us criticising ourselves and obsessing over false beliefs. So, left unchecked, your inner critic creates a mental pattern of negative commentary. This can undermine your health, demolishes your creativity, and destroys your spontaneity. That critic loves to attack the work you're just beginning and it wants you to stop moving forward.

For example, if you don't go to the gym, it tells you that you're not very serious about exercising, but when you do go to the gym it wants you to know that you're not very good at this kind of workout and should have just stayed home.

The hallmark of your inner critic is that it criticises, no matter what you do. If you don't recognise this, you'll give it way too much power. It is simply a single voice among many. Yet it just happens to be one of the loudest ones, so let's talk about a few ways that we can overcome it.

Don't argue with it.

It's a losing battle, so don't engage with it. That voice is always based in fear and not in rational thinking, so it's not going to fight with you in a rational way.

Name it.

Even if you think that sounds silly, the minute you name something, you take away some of its power because this gives it a form; it's no longer a nameless dread that you can't quite identify. Actively notice when this voice is chiming in and especially what it's ringing really loudly. Call it by its new name, like Gonzo.

Question it.

Learning to question that voice in your head helps you begin to understand the difference between the inner critic voice you developed in childhood and the realistic voice you have now. Your inner critic thinks very much in black or white—right or wrong, yes or no—while the realistic voice thinks in shades of gray. The inner critic is repetitive and nags you in a berating tone, telling you there's no way this is going to work. Your realistic voice looks at clues to decide, yes this will work, or says,

'Yeah, I don't know. Maybe we need to redirect and figure something else out'. It will try to address the issues instead of dismissing everything, and it speaks in a much kinder tone. Finding even one contradiction to what your inner critic is saying can make it lose its power over you.

Review.

Become aware and review your mistakes, and then move on. We don't want to allow that inner critic to take hold, to use that remote control in our head to play that negative movie loop over and over again. That just allows us to nitpick ourselves. We only need to review our past mistakes once or twice to learn from them, and then move on. This takes power away from your inner critic, and when it has less energy it starts to weaken and eventually goes away.

Praise yourself.

You need to change your relationship with praise. This may seem very counterintuitive, or you may not want to praise yourself. Examine how you feel about praise, especially if you're a high achiever. You might be used to the gold stars and the amazing reviews. You might be used to working with clients who are wowed by what you do. But this praise can become addictive, and we may become reliant on it, allowing it to fulfill us and define us.

When we find ourselves in that loop, we might be afraid of moving on. Because we're in this loop of wanting and craving more praise, we're afraid of what our inner critic is going to say. This can stop us from innovating, from trying new things, or from going after what we want. Know that your self-worth *has* to come from within— you're already enough.

Be present.

Become still and present and the inner critic loses traction, because it feeds on the past and the mistakes we've made and the fears of the future. When you're really enjoying everything as it is, right now in the moment, you can let the voices of your inner critic come and go. Acknowledge them and thank them for their inputs, and ask them to move along.

Here's the thing. Your inner critic loves to ruin the show. It will never be completely quiet, but if you can acknowledge it and really focus on the present, on what you're enjoying doing, it really does lose its power over you.

Reclaim your inner power, Princess.

YOU ARE NOT YOUR EGO

I'm reading through posts in a group that I love, full of awesome women focusing on their money mindsets. Every day there are several posts by these women sharing small wins or huge ones, big a-ha moments and many moments of suffering, fear, frustration—basically all the feels on their way to finding financial freedom.

What I love about it is that this is not a self-promotion group; it's a 'sharing your real-life journey' group. It's both inspiring and real. Most times I go in to read or contribute, I come away feeling filled up on possibility and excitement.

Except for the time I see a post from a coach who's celebrating an honest win of already making well over $200,000 in a launch that's not even really started being promoted yet. I'm instantly deflated. I notice how triggered I am. I see the comments from others celebrating her and congratulating her.

I give it a heart, but deep down I'm jealous. I'm frustrated. And clearly I'm triggered. What's more, my ego is hurting.

What is ego? Ego is your self-image of who you are. It's the thoughts and emotions that you identify with. It's the beliefs that you think are rock solid and completely true. It's what you think reality is like, even if it's not true at all.

The irony is that several years before, I did a launch that netted me $250,000 and I was beyond thrilled when I made my big vision all happen, just like this lady had. So why was I here right now, telling myself a completely different story that wasn't even remotely true? Because over the past few years, I'd slipped into more subconscious thinking and hadn't been keeping my ego in check.

The problem is that the ego is clingy and it is adept at self-preservation. What it does, especially if you're trying to get ahead in life, is attempt to hold you back. It doesn't want a gorgeous Princess like yourself to go out into the big wide world and realise your unlimited potential.

Your ego has been built up since you were a kid, and the fact is that the notion you have of who you are right now is totally fictitious, an illusion. It's what your ego has led you to believe.

Hang on a minute, I hear you saying. How on earth did this ego come about then?

It evolved through the experiences that you had in early childhood and early adulthood all the way up to now. Every experience that you had, through your whole life from birth to this current second, has added something to your ego.

In that moment I was describing, it was the ego that was responsible for me instantly telling myself why I'm not capable of getting that same result as that lady in the group had. The ego was the one belittling me for playing it small, tormenting me for being jealous.

Your ego is insecure. It needs approval. It needs validation. It needs you to look good. But the one thing you need to stop doing is feeding it!

When I started comparing myself with her and then got frustrated at myself for doing that—yep, you guessed it, that's my ego.

I imagine that, like me, you let the ego run your life, and your perception of reality too, more often than you want to admit.

SO LET'S DECONSTRUCT THE EGO AND LOOSEN ITS CONTROL ON US.

You are so much more than your ego allows you or wants you to be, so here's my example of what you can do.

I drop down to the yoga mat and breathe through a series of flow movements I feel like doing in the moment. Then I sit on the couch and take time to pause and really look at myself.

Wait a hot damn minute, I say to myself in my head, that's your ego talking, Natalie, not the truth. Time to tell your ego to bugger off. Then I mime the action of reaching into my head, pulling this ego figure out, and placing it on my hand, outside of my mind and body.

I observe it, and smile. Oh there you are, my friend. Doing your best to protect me, by keeping my emotions in check. Attempting to make me feel lesser than, so you can keep me from getting hurt, and protect me from dreaming big.

I have enough self-awareness to separate what is clearly a lie from the truth, and I get honest with myself about what really just happened. I say to myself, 'Nat, you realise this is your own creation, you've made all this up, but the great news is, you can also undo this. Even if you don't know how, you'll figure it out'.

This instantly makes me feel better, because I'm not forcing myself to come up with the how, just to acknowledge that I've got this.

Then I ask myself, 'What do I need to let go of here that's holding me back?' Even though it's hard, I start to see that what came up for me, like it always does, is that feeling of *I'm not enough*. I've told myself I'm not capable of achieving this kind of success myself.

I smile to myself again. So *not* true, Nat.

I then look at this situation once again, from a neutral space, and this time I get really curious. What do I really see as the truth here?

I realise that I'm actually really thrilled for this lady, and super excited that she's achieved this. And I'm excited that I'm totally able and willing to achieve this too.

I feel more abundant. There's more than enough of this to go around. I start to feel this buzz in my body full of genuine excitement for her. She had a vision, she's making it happen, and it's truly inspiring. The buzz amplifies as I realise I'm getting excited for her *and* me. This is what I want.

This is how I want to feel too when I have an amazing launch. I really sink into that feeling as if it's happening to me and damn, it feels good! My mind races along, visualising me during an amazing launch, feeling incredible, and abundant, and I align the feelings in my body to the intentions in my mind.

All of this takes less than five minutes, and in that time my ego has truly left the building, and what's left is simply me. Me in my wholeness, me as who I really am. I'm free. I'm excited. I'm operating on a whole new level. That's because I've gone from someone who's been unconsciously repeating a pattern of beating myself up, to someone who's consciously chosen to become aware that I can do anything I desire, and put my thoughts and intentions into fully.

I'm the master of my mind; it is not the master of me.

The crazy thing is, you and I go through our whole day, week, and life like this. We're constantly letting our ego take over. We go through life playing this up-and-down game. It's a game of chasing after things that are good and avoiding the things that are bad. But that ain't gonna get you living in your truth, gorgeous.

You need to step into the present moment, and simply be *you*. When you start to do this, you move away from constantly judging yourself (and others), and move toward what you want, and more importantly how you want to *feel*.

You become more at peace, calmer, and more of your natural 'you'. You raise your level of consciousness. That's ultimately what ego is about. It's about raising your level of consciousness.

The more you practice retraining your mind and interrupting those pesky and damaging limiting self-beliefs and stories you've been telling yourself ever since you were in diapers, the more you can step fully into your beautiful, powerful, and whole self.

Goodbye, ego. Hello to the real, whole, complete, and amazing *you*!

WEED OUT THOSE NEGATIVE THOUGHTS

Did you know that we humans have 60,000 thoughts a day? 60,000? I mean, what the heck! Our minds are working overtime. What's more, research shows that 90% of those thoughts are the same thoughts as the day before, and even worse, they're either neutral or negative.

What a bummer! That means the same thoughts will always lead to the same choices. The same choices will always create the same behaviours, the same behaviours will produce the same experiences, and those same experiences will create the same emotions and drive the exact same thoughts.

Our thoughts create our reality. Every day we get to choose the reality we wish for ourselves. We get to choose what we think, how we act, and how we feel. Life is meant to be lived to the fullest, yet when we wake up in the morning, we're already worrying about things! We have doubts, fears, criticisms, and thoughts of all the things that went wrong yesterday and could go wrong today.

We grab our mobile phones and they confirm this is true—depressing or fear-inducing news stories, addictive social media that makes us compare ourselves to others before we've even gotten out of bed, so that we now feel woefully inadequate. To add to that, we've got thoughts about our relationships, or people who bother us, about our frustrations, anger, resentment, and all kinds of other things.

And that's what most of us wake up with. No wonder it can feel easier to stay in bed and put your head under the covers. But wouldn't it be far better to wake up with the truest version of who we are, and how we want to behave, and show up in the world to live our best life?

I think so. So it's time to think outside the box to get those neurons firing differently.

A few years ago I did some learning about negative thoughts. A fascinating fact is that when scientists track such thoughts with brain scans, they can literally watch the thought grow. Turns out positive thoughts only begin to grow after being 'held in the brain' or focused on for 15 seconds.

Let that sink in for a moment. It takes zero time for our brains to process and believe negative thoughts and 15 seconds for it to process positive ones. And this increases if you grew up in a negative environment.

IT'S TIME TO TAKE UP GARDENING.

Say what, Natalie?

Yep, you heard me right. Negative thoughts, if left unchecked, can literally take over our mind. If you don't consistently weed your lovely garden, you will never see the flowers bloom. As a keen gardener, I've had times when I let too many weeds grow in my garden. And damn, do those weeds grow quickly and cover everything, taking over all the plants and flowers and choking them.

Pulling out the weeds is just as important as what you plant in your garden. Once you've planted your lovely dahlias, you need to give them the right environment to thrive. They need sunshine, shelter, water, nutrients, and I'm sure they'd love it if you sang to them too.

The mind is also a place to be nurtured and designed by you. If your mind is full of weeds, it's full of confusion. There's no focus; there's no vision there. And you're allowing the weeds to dominate everything you think, and smother your hopes and dreams.

The more we clean up our mind garden and remove all those weeds, so to speak, the more we can fill our mind with the thoughts and visions for our best possible life. We also need to carefully guard our mind and make sure to remove the negative thoughts as quickly as possible, to make way for the reality we want. This means working on adopting a positive, growth mindset, and then feeding it more of the right messages and thoughts to strengthen this every day.

So go and read those law of attraction books, watch those motivational video montages on YouTube, do your mantras, and write out and read your affirmations. Avoid the energy vampires, the drama queens, and the naysayers, and hang out with the people who inspire you and energise you.

If this is all you feed your mind every day, it's what your mind will adopt and believe.

IF YOU WANT TO CHANGE YOUR LIFE, START WITH CHANGING YOUR THOUGHTS.

In the wise words of author and consultant Dr Joe Dispenza, your mind does not actually know the difference between a real thought and something that you are envisioning. Your mind also has an incredible visual component and if you close your eyes each morning, and meditate and be fully present on the vision of how you want to live your life, that is actually what your mind believes to be true.

So you can imagine your future self right now as if it's happening. And guess what—your mind starts to believe that this is the reality. And that is actually the future that you tend toward, and it becomes true a lot more quickly than you think.

I know this to be true. When I created my first Life Canvas—a holistic vision you wish for three years from now, but written and drawn in the present tense—60% of what I wanted came true in the first year! Because I was so focused on that vision, consciously and subconsciously I opened myself up to opportunities that would make it possible.

The universe was like 'Dang Natalie, I'm glad you got so clear on what you want. Now I'm going to start delivering it to you, okay?'

My clients experience the same thing when they use my Life Canvas. They turn to me and say, 'OMG, I didn't realise it would start happening that quickly. What do I do?'

Not a bad problem to have, in my opinion. I say, 'Go for it!'

BACK TO THE REAL GOLD.

So if you are what you think, then surely you ought to be thinking about the best possible version of you and the life that you want, right? The more you think about that, and the more you feel it and connect it with your heart, your mind, your soul, the more likely that is actually to become your true reality.

Everything starts to shift in you; the universe starts to answer your calls. The energy that you're putting out is starting to radiate, and it affects others.

You know when you meet those people and they just look like they're on cloud nine, like they're high on life? Like they're living on purpose? It's because they are, it's because they see their vision and hold it so strongly and live it every day, that their vision has actually become their reality. And that's how they operate and behave. And consequently, every single thing in their life starts to compound and come true. Then it becomes their daily reality.

Imagine having no doubts, no fears, but instead being able to control your mind with exactly what you want to be thinking about, and push yourself toward that greater vision. Doesn't that sound a whole lot better than focusing on the past, on the negative thoughts and the things that you did wrong and things that 'might have been'?

If we wake up every single morning thinking about the past, guess what? Our past suddenly becomes our reality today. We're stuck in a frickin' endless cycle of crap. If that sounds like you, you need to interrupt that way of thinking. It starts with being very present with yourself, aligning yourself, closing your eyes, and sitting still.

SIT FOR A MOMENT, WILL YOU?

Five minutes, ten minutes, or more. Breathe deeply and envision that future. Continue to focus when your thoughts shift to the negative or distract you. Bring it back to that vision and just be there in the here and now.

It's time to pull out those weeds, plant some beautiful new roses, sweet peas, and gerberas and bring the most fantastic garden to life, in full bloom. It makes me so happy to look at flowers, and to stop and smell the roses. Imagine how much your mind is going to love you for doing the same to your thoughts.

Start digging, lady. There's gold to be found in that mind of yours.

PART 2

CREATE YOUR UNIVERSE

As your inner heroine now knows from Part 1, the way in which you live in this world is entirely up to you. It's time to unleash her now to bend reality your way. This is about meshing the power of your thoughts, intentions, and mindset with the real-world situations you'll find yourself in, so that you can weave your magic, and live life on your own terms.

KNOW YOUR WHY

Why do you do what you do?

No, really. *Why* do you do what you do, day in and day out? Or to rephrase, why *aren't* you doing the things you say you love to do most?

The truth is, the defining factor that separates people who live a life of purpose that gets them springing out of bed every day is that they know their why. These people succeed because they are so crystal clear on their why, and they're committed to it. They live and breathe it.

Sure, they may annoy the hell out of you with their incredible levels of energy, and endless enthusiasm, drive, and determination to see their why through, but deep down you want some of what she's having. And you want it now, bitch!

And there's a good reason to get your own why in order. It's going to serve you on the days when inspiration leaves you for dust. When willpower packs up and leaves. Neither inspiration nor willpower stick around when things get hard, or you lose momentum or feel like giving up. They're fleeting at best. A bit like having an affair, all hot and steamy, but the ecstasy and joy don't last long; reality soon hits that it's over and that person was merely an exciting distraction.

You must have something that is going to motivate you to push past every single obstacle you're going to face, every challenge thrown at you, every time your inner critic gets the best of you.

As you well know, anybody can start, but most people don't actually finish what they set out to do. One of the key ways to finish what you start is to align everything you do with your why, your purpose in life. The stronger and clearer it is, the more you will embody it, and the more certain you are to unleash your superwoman powers and your fearless determination to realise your why, and make it a reality.

WHY IS THAT?

One of my all-time favourite TED talks is by one of my heroes, Simon Sinek, motivational speaker and author of *Start with Why,* among other books. Sinek believes that every person knows what it is they do, that some of us know how we do it, but very few of us have ever really taken the time to think about why we do what we do.

He believes that those who are clear on their why are the ones who never give up and go on to succeed.

The *why* is about our contribution to impact and serve others. The *why* inspires us. In short, your why is your purpose. It's the love of your life. It won't leave you in the morning, with just a lingering kiss and a promise of more.

In fact, it provides a clear answer to these questions: Why do I get out of bed every morning? Why does my business exist? Why should that matter to anyone else?

What's even better is that the more you share your why with others, the more they believe in you and your why, and that leads them to align with you, trust you, purchase your products, seek your services, or hire you to help them.

The flip side of this is that if you don't know *why* you do what you do, how can you expect anyone else to know? For others to know your why, you must first be clear on your own why, but how exactly does one do that?

CREATING YOUR *WHY* STATEMENT

Your *why* statement is a sentence that clearly expresses your unique *contribution* and *impact*.

Let's break that down:

1. The *impact* reflects the difference you want to make in the world.

2. The *contribution* is the primary action that you take toward making your impact.

To begin outlining your why statement, you have to think about what it is you want to contribute to the world at large. One you've identified your contribution, you have to figure out what you want the impact of your contribution to be. For example, my why statement is as follows:

To show women how to unlock their potential and use it to get paid to do what they love, so that they live a truly rewarding and abundant life, lifting other women up to do the same.

—NATALIE SISSON

While there's no one path for discovering your life's purpose, there are many ways you can gain greater insight into yourself, and a larger perspective on what it is that you have to offer the world when you know why you're doing something.

Understanding what drives and motivates us can completely change the trajectory of our lives. When you are clear on your why it enables you to focus your efforts on what matters most, compelling you to take risks and push forward despite the obstacles and hurdles that may arise.

WHEN YOU KNOW YOUR WHY, YOU CANENDURE ANY HOW.

I'll be 100% honest with you here. My why didn't just jump out at me one day and say, 'Here I am, Natalie!' And yours won't do that either. It may come to you in a fit of inspiration, while reading this book, or it might take some deep soul searching about what is really important to you.

It really depends how much inner work you've been doing, and how much time you allow yourself to connect to what you feel, not just what you think. It's a process, and one that you need to invest time into. But it's oh so worth it. I know from experience that my why acts as my true North Star. It guides me in *every* area of my life and work, every decision I make, every action I take.

I didn't appreciate why that was (see what I did there?), until I heard Sinek state that the best thing about your why is that it's a biological constant. It has nothing to do with what you do. It's based on the biology of how you make decisions and what drives you and motivates you, which means that it doesn't matter what stage of life you're at, or what industry you're in.

All you need to do is have the will and the desire to want to understand what drives and inspires you. If you can't see it, smell it, taste it, or feel it move you deeply in your soul, then you're not going to go after it with all it takes.

It has to be deeply personal to you. When your why is enough, it will help you move mountains, baby. If it's not, it will be the reason you:

- Keep *not* showing up for yourself

- Let procrastination win the day

- Don't play full out in your business

- Stay stuck in a vicious cycle of mediocre

- Keep beating yourself up for not doing 'all' the things

To recap, my why is:

To show women how to unlock their potential and use it to get paid to do what they love, so that they live a truly rewarding and abundant life, lifting other women up to do the same.

—NATALIE SISSON

For me, my why is really clear and energising. It's so powerful that I will often roll onto my yoga mat first thing in the morning, and start thinking about all the women I want to lift up and celebrate that day.

My why is strongly embedded into my business mission, which is:

To lead 1,000 women to earn $10,000+ per month and donate at least 1% of that to a cause or charity that is dear to their heart, and in doing so creating a ripple effect in other women's lives.

The thing is, I put metrics in here to make it tangible, but the why is not actually about the money. Underlying this mission is the financial, mindset, and lifestyle freedom that comes from building a business that pays you what you're worth, and makes an impact. It's not about the $10K a month in income; that's great, but it's really about who you need to become, and what beliefs you need to hold, in order to earn that, and beyond.

It can take a while, and require deep reflection and a process to define a mission, but damn, it's worth it when you do. I came up with mine while sitting on an indoor bike trainer in our barn, listening to a call about business strategy, and I was struck with inspiration in the moment as to what my why was.

I leant over (still strapped into my indoor bike trainer) to write on the whiteboard, which fortunately was in arm's reach, and scribbled out a mission that came pouring out of me.

Since defining this and stating it, I've talked about it on my podcast, in my emails, in my blogs, on social, to my friends, family, peers, community, and clients. It's permeated my inner world and extended into every aspect of my outer world—including my messaging, my vision, my work, my offerings, my values, my website, my coaching, and where I put my energy.

Everything changed when I got clear on this, and while making this mission a reality is likely five or so years in the making, it's given me the North-Star guidance and purpose I so desired. It's led to my most favourite creation to date—the $10K Club, which in turn has led to the most wonderful women being attracted to join me, and be part of this mission just by doing so.

In fact, it's what I teach in the very first lesson of my $10K Club framework to new members because it's that important.

So, what's your why?

BE PROACTIVE VERSUS REACTIVE

Fun Fact: This book was born in a pandemic. I started my book crowdfunding campaign during the most uncertain and shocking time for most of the world, when a new reality was dawning that COVID-19 was in fact a pandemic.

It felt like literally the hardest time ever for me to show up and ask people to preorder my book, at a time when everyone was in shock, and what's more on a book with a title that could either be deemed entirely relevant to our situation, or completely insensitive.

I then wrote this entire book during this crisis, through months of lockdown and hundreds of thousands of lives lost, through conspiracy theories, through the world tackling institutional racism and heading into a global economic recession like none experienced before.

This proved to me that anything can be done, despite all odds, when you have the right mindset and the best intentions. During the pandemic, more than ever, my 'infinite' mindset served me incredibly well.

I chose the proactive route over the reactive route. As an eternal optimist, I chose to see potential versus panic. As a result, this period turned out to be my most productive and successful, both personally and professionally.

I want to share how to adopt this infinite mindset in your life too, because when the shit hits the fan—and you know it's gonna—time and time again, it's going to be your best ally.

KEEP CALM AND STAY THE COURSE

During this same time I saw countless influencers and online entrepreneurs go into panic mode and really ratchet up their offers, feeding on the fear, and probably experiencing fear themselves.

I saw others come out and drop everything to make stuff to help people out, because wherever you looked there were stories of people losing jobs, businesses shutting down, and people's livelihoods coming to an abrupt end. Many people were in a really tough place.

Initially I was inspired by them, and I started doing the same myself, thinking about what I could offer, repurpose, reignite that would help people most. I had ideas pouring out of me.

After a while, I realised I felt exhausted, getting caught up in all this reactive energy, rather than being proactive, staying focused on the priorities that make the most profit, the most impact, and reach the right people.

I moved into one of our guest bedrooms, set up a desk, and got to work. I relished having no external activities, meetings, or events so that for the first time in ages, I could just focus in and turn up to serve my community and make magic happen.

I realised that what I teach—how to get paid to be you, using your unique combination of skills, experience, and knowledge; and packaging that into online products, digital courses, and services—was needed more now than ever.

I felt the need to show up and serve and do it right away. I knew this was the place and time that I could truly help. This is what I've been preaching and teaching for ten years of running an online business from anywhere, with multiple revenue streams, that lets you get paid to simply be *you*.

And I'd seen too many of my friends, peers, and complete strangers have their businesses ripped out from underneath them, because their business model left them super exposed and with just one source of income.

I released a podcast episode in mid-April 2020, when most countries around the world were realising the full extent of what this pandemic would bring if we weren't able to control it. Most of us were in some form of lockdown or quarantine. Everything was uncertain.

Here's a piece of what I shared that really resonated with my community, and served as a huge turning point for me at the time, as I actually took my own advice for once!

> I know it can be tempting right now to throw everything up in the air, and get to work creating an offer or service that you could release as quickly as possible to help people in their time of need.
>
> Or resurrect an old course or offer, that might actually land really well right now with your customers, earn you some money, and make you feel like you're doing something useful.
>
> I get it. Oh I soooo get it. In the last two weeks I've felt called to show up and serve others more than ever.
>
> In my work as a business coach who focuses on how to get paid to be you, I've had *all* the ideas on how I can most quickly pivot, create, and release helpful courses or programs right now. How I can reach those entrepreneurs whose revenues have been slashed or who have lost their jobs or livelihoods overnight.
>
> I was working on this, while pouring energy into my book crowdfunding campaign and welcoming in all

the lovely students who chose the 'Write Your Damn Book' reward level to join me live over 60 days.

I was showing up. I was going live on Facebook and Instagram, putting out blog posts to share my knowledge and help and talking to amazing guests on my podcasts to help my community find the silver lining in all of this.

I was getting drawn to all these ideas and possible ways that I could help, and I wasn't focusing on the one thing I needed to, which was my mission.

And I realised I need to stop, refocus, and come back to it.

My mission is to lead 1,000 women to earn $10K per month and donate at least 1% of their profit to a cause of their choice, and in doing so, create a ripple effect in other women's lives.

The minute I focused back on that, I realised they are the people who I want to serve. I realised that all the ideas I had thought about putting out an offer for were targeted at beginners who have lost their job, or are trying to start a business, or people who have side hustles, or just starting out.

I've spent years serving the beginners, and as much as I love them, catering to them wasn't going to serve my mission. What's more, there were countless others already helping those people.

I knew it was time to step up and serve women who are already in business, who are already making an impact, who are already on their path to what they desire, and they're willing to invest.

They've been in business a few years and they're smart, capable, and ready to be and do more. They have big dreams and desires along with decent incomes, but it's not consistent.

They have great months, and then they have terrible months. Nothing is ever certain or in flow. They're not reaching their revenue goals and they are also working way too hard. Yet they need more than just a great business plan and sticking to it. They need to focus on their priorities, put key systems, funnels, and a team in place, and get clear on their why.

Then they will absolutely be able to skyrocket their business and their own confidence. I knew that to do all that, more than anything, they needed the right mindset to be able to scale their business, earn what they're worth, and the right mentoring and community to help them unleash their potential.

And then they are able to step into their power and greatness and have a massive impact on other women's lives, creating a beautiful circular economy of women lifting up other women.

Yes, I thought to myself, those are my women. Those are my Queens!

I felt more on purpose, more productive, and more focused than ever, and I got to work designing a framework upon which I could build the best offering ever.

I had a vision. I had a plan and I stuck to it, because I knew in that moment, I needed to be a North Star for myself as much as for the Queens I wanted to serve.

I knew that in the heart of the chaos, fear, and uncertainty, even if it felt completely dire, with the right vision and plan I could continue to build the business that I loved, that supported the life I wanted and made the impact I most want to see in this world, and that I could do this for hundreds of other women, too.

Creatives, coaches, consultants, and service-based businesses—this is your time to step up, stay true to your plan, and continue to help your customers in the way that you do best.

Pivot if it's necessary, make an offer that could dramatically help or impact others in a positive way, if you need.

But stay focused on doing what you do well, with the resources you have, and the time that you have, to keep on showing up and providing.

Don't take advantage of people who are des-perate. Don't market like crazy to people who are vulnerable.

How you show up and act right now is how you will be remembered for a long time.

So make sure you come from a place of integrity, generosity, compassion, and genuine value creation.

Reflect and ask yourself, are you being proactive or reactive?

I got a lot of listener feedback. They told me my message was a voice of reason, in amongst the frenzy.

People shared their stories with me on Messenger and via email, letting me know that after listening, they too were taking a step back, to take stock, and really listen to how they felt, and to their intuition. Some chose to step back completely and rest, that this was the break they needed. Others felt more focused, and back on track to come from a place of love, empathy, understanding, and service.

'Twas a beautiful thing to see these proactive women step into their power.

So what about you? No matter what's happening in your life, or outside of it, what can you do to come from a place of proactiveness, rather than reactiveness?

Hint: Take a deep breath, then come back to your why, what you value most, and start there. You already have the answer within you.

BUILD YOUR MOAT

In fairy tales, most princesses live in a castle. Some castles, the really fortified ones, have moats—a body of water that encircles the castle. This makes it harder for the enemy to attack because they have to navigate across the often dark and deep waters, which gives the guards protecting the castle time to fend off an attack.

In short, they're pretty handy.

I learned years ago that, if I want to do my best work and live a life I truly desire, I need a really big frickin' moat around me. In other words, I need to create and honour my boundaries.

These boundaries protect me from:

- Giving away too much of my energy

- Working too hard

- Letting negative people into my life

- Overconsuming social media

- Getting stressed out

- Taking on too many projects or responsibilities

- Getting involved in other people's business or drama

- Putting other peoples' needs before me

- Getting poor sleeps

- Not prioritising my rest

- Being too accessible to clients, friends, and family.

The truth is, as a high performer and an overachiever, I'm prone to pushing too hard, too often. This is something I'm finally learning to manage, by adopting the mantra 'ease, grace, and flow' every single day.

There is no one else here to look to but me. The buck stops with me. Change starts with me. If I forget to look after myself, in order to look out for and help others, I pay the price.

In 2019, I had single-handedly said yes too to many things (read the chapter 'The Power of Saying No'). I mean I'm not the only princess with a lot on her plate, but this was ridiculous. I had taken on a four-day-a-week job (my first one in ten years), another part-time contract on a new business I couldn't resist being part of, and had squeezed my business into just one day a week, including launching a new course.

To cap it off, I was training six days a week for my Half Ironman triathlon and fitting that in early morning or evening.

Craziness. And I think I'm a smart person! Really, Nat?

When I operate at this level, I learn a new lesson, or seven. Every. Single. Time. I take it on board. I apply it. And I make changes. But these are expensive lessons to learn.

I preach to my people all the time, you're not superwoman. You're super, but you're not a superhero with special powers that make you invincible. And for lovers of Marvel and DC Comics, you'll know superheroes have their downsides, their vulnerabilities, and their shite days too.

You and I need to acknowledge this and put in place boundaries to protect our super-ness. 'Cos no one else will or can, but you.

You need to build your freaking moat.

Here are my hard-learned lessons on creating a moat that protects your most precious resources—your time and energy—and empowers others to do what they need, to allow you to do less.

Firstly, let people know when you're open for business.

Even if you're not in business for yourself, the principles still apply. Tell people when you are available, and when you're not.

For example, I aim to work five hours per day, from 8 a.m. to 1 p.m. Those are the times my team know that I'm online and responding to them in Slack (for quick communications and short conversations) and Asana for priority tasks and project work. Note that we don't use email. That's reserved for clients, customers, and business inquiries or opportunities.

I also check in again around 5 p.m. to plan for the next day and make sure everyone has what they need to move forward. Because my team is global, some are just starting their day while others are finishing up. We don't work weekends and I do not expect them to reply or respond to me then, and unless they want to, I don't expect them to work evenings. It's up to them to manage their time and work.

Same applies at home. Especially if you have a home office, you need a sign on the door that says when it's appropriate to come in, and when you're busy. I like using the sign 'On air', which signals I'm doing a podcast interview, or on a group coaching call. It's fun too.

Set clear times for contact.

This is critical. Set clear times for your clients, peers, colleagues, and loved ones to call, text, or message you. You can make these certain windows throughout the day, or make it easy with no calls until after 1 p.m., for example.

Same goes with booking in time to speak with you. Use a calendar scheduling tool like Calendly to block in times for specific activities. I have two half days a month for guests to book in on my podcast, and half a day a week for client calls or application calls. The rest of the time is usually unavailable because I have calendar-blocked the heck out of my week and month.

I have set times for team calls, for strategy work, for content creation, for financial and operational decisions, for admin and for learning. No one gets to book in when I'm doing yoga first thing in the morning, or taking a hike or going for a run in the afternoon. I block out lunch, dinner, and free time to do whatever the heck I want.

Choose your prime communication tool.

Choose *one* messaging tool that *you* prefer, and tell people to contact you on that. Otherwise you know you're gonna receive communications on WhatsApp, Voxer, Signal, Messenger, and email, at a bare minimum! And who the heck can keep up with that? More importantly, who needs to?

Reiterate this regularly, as well as when they can expect a response:

- If it's non-urgent, message me on Signal. I will do my best to respond within 24 hours.

- If it's very important, call my mobile, and if I don't answer, then text me. I will do my best to get back to you within the hour.

- If it's urgent, call my mobile, and if I don't answer, hang up and call twice more. I will respond as soon as possible.

This trains people to know what they can expect, and minimise the amount of confusion, hurt, and lost in translation moments, simply because you set clear boundaries.

Institute email protection.

The same deal applies here. Block out time to check your email, then honour your calendar and don't give in. I know I have the best days when I don't check email until late morning, or even after lunch. I have the worst days when I keep it open, and respond to everything as it comes in, feeling like I'm doing something useful, when in fact I'm procrastinating!

Have an autoresponder that reiterates the times you're available and not available, your rules around non-urgent and urgent, and your turnaround time for responses. At the time of this writing, my partner, Josh, changed his autoresponder from 'I only check email once a week, so best to message me on Slack if you want a reply sooner' to saying he only checks it every three weeks!

Better yet, hire a virtual assistant for email and calendar management and watch your life transform in an instant as you realise it really wasn't as important as you thought, and they've got the majority of your emails handled, leaving you with the ones that truly matter.

Once a month, if I'm not regularly hitting inbox zero from ruthless email triage, I archive every message I've been keeping in my inbox. Why? If it was important I would have dealt with it by now, this is poor use of my inbox, and if it was important to them, they would have followed up already. Easy.

DIGITAL DETOX DAYS

Every week I enjoy my Freedom Friday. This falls on a Friday, no surprises there, and is a non-workday. As in I don't go into my office or near my laptop. I often hide my phone in the wardrobe too. Yes, I hide it so I can find it, but the old 'out of sight, out of mind' really works. So does realising you have to walk more than an arm's length distance to retrieve it. We humans are notoriously lazy. Oh, and put it in airplane mode too.

The point is, I enjoy a digital-free day, where I'm connected to just one thing, being present. That means heading out in nature, playing with the dogs, reading a book in the sun, painting, gardening, socialising with friends. Whatever I wish.

Depending on how I feel, I reserve the right to do learning on my iPad, which has no work tools or apps on it, just entertainment and access to courses that will help me expand my mind or acquire new skills or insights.

If you can't do this during the week, then allocate at least one day on the weekend to do this for yourself. The first time will be hard. Likely really hard, so enlist help. Have someone kidnap your phone, unplug the Wi-Fi, or better yet, come pick you up for a day's outing, without your phone.

Once you realise the joy of the space, time, and energy you get back in abundance, you'll wonder why you haven't done this all along. Fun fact: I get my best business, house, and personal growth ideas on detox days.

POWER OF THREE

Thanks to LifePilot, a powerful yet simple methodology and tool Josh and I created to turn our dreams into reality, we use the power of three for everything. We set no more than three most important actions or intentions each day, week, month, quarter, and year.

Why three? More than that and you're simply setting yourself up for failure. Plus, if you can't cull your to-dos until you're left with three that will truly move the needle for you, you most likely need help. I genuinely mean that in the loveliest possible way; remember that superhero statement early on?

What I'm really talking about here is valuing your time and energy so much that you funnel it into three things that will make everything else pale into insignificance.

Using my colour-coded LifePilot spreadsheet that I love, a day might look like this:

- **Work:** Batch record two podcast interviews—*win for planning ahead.*

- **Personal:** Finish final module of financial mastery course—*win for knowledge acquisition.*

- **Lifestyle:** Go on a lovely river walk with the pooches—*win for revitalising my energy and creative juices, plus dog love.*

Over a week that would look like:

- **Impact:** Write the next chapter of my book—*win for taking action and making progress toward publishing.*

- **Relationship:** Plan out next two long weekends with Josh—*win for connection time with my love and visioning what lights us up and lets us dream big.*

- **Health:** Do at least three triathlon training sessions—*win for consistent training and improvement before an event.*

In a month, all these activities would tie in to the three main goals I set:

- **Impact:** Get first rough draft book into editor for feedback—*win for bite-size chunks to motivate me to keep writing, and a deadline to work toward.*

- **Work:** Release pilot launch of course on podcasting how-to—*win for using podcast interviews, and being interviewed to come up with great course content to pre-promote.*

- **Financial:** Finish course and implement upgrades with accountant—*win for working toward improving my financial literacy, along* *with building a better relationship with my accountant and enlisting their expertise.*

Important: You set your annual goals across the eight areas of life that are most important (check out lifepilot. co for these), then transfer those to your quarterly goals or intentions, then break them down into your monthly, weekly, and daily goals. Easy!

These are only some of the main ways to build your moat, and I'm pretty sure you know, deep down, all the ways in which you can become the master of your own day, that you simply need to put in place.

The massive upside is that instead of seeing the stressed-out, snappy, always busy, frazzled version of you, everyone will get a much better look at the real you—the happy, relaxed, calm, joyful, organised, stress-free version.

Go make it happen, Princess!

THE POWER OF SAYING NO

'Would you like to babysit my kids tomorrow night?'

'Yes—yes, sure.'

'Would you like to take on that extra project because I'm too lazy to do it at work and you're the only person who takes up the slack?'

'Yes—okay, yes'.

'Would you like to go to that event with me tomorrow night to network even though you really freaking hate doing that?'

'Okay, yes—I'd love to'.

Are you *kidding* me?

If these are the kinds of things you say yes to even when you don't want to, I urge you to stop doing that right now. Instead, pause, take a breath, and say, 'No, thank you'.

Saying no is a very, very powerful response to things that don't feel in alignment with you, things that make you tense up inside and feel so icky. Then why is it so freaking hard to say no?

Clearly, you should not be doing things you absolutely can't stand to do. I'm talking about the stuff you have no desire to do with all of your heart and soul, but you wind up doing it anyway. Why? Because you simply can't say the word *no* (which, by the way, has one fewer letter than *yes*, so it's even easier to say!).

Your inability to say no when you most want to is the reason you are doing all these things in your life that don't serve you and frankly don't serve others either.

So how do you get past this?

Step One: Try it out.

Go stand in front of the mirror and practice saying no. I kid you not! Watch your reaction when you say the word. Do you wince? Do you giggle? Do avoid looking yourself in the eye? If you do any of that, you have a serious 'yes problem' that we need to fix. But it's fixable and it will absolutely change your life!

I remember the first time I put out a high-level coaching package, and I stood in front of the mirror several times, saying out loud, 'That will be $10,000', without laughing, sniggering, or looking uncomfortable.

That's because it *really* works. It prepares you mentally for getting comfortable with what you're about to say, and more importantly for believing it. Do it daily if you need to, and especially before you're going to meet up with someone you simply can't ever seem to say no to.

If the mirror trick isn't working, practice with a friend: get them to ask you a series of questions you can say no to and keep going until saying no becomes natural to you. That way, the next time somebody makes a request of you that simply does not light you up, you can turn to them and say, 'No, but thank you'.

Let's try that again! Turn to them and say, 'No, but thank you'. You don't even need to smile. Just let your response rest and then watch and observe their response.

It might be 'What?!' or 'Oh...oh, I see...' or maybe 'Are you sure?'

To which you get to say, 'Yes, I'm sure, and no, thank you'.

Try it out when responding to the next request from a colleague, a friend, your mother, your sister, your father, a 'lover from your other brutha'. You know at least one of those people. Try it out on them because it's important to practice the art of saying no—there's a lot of nuance to it.

WHAT ELSE IS BEHIND THE ART OF SAYING NO?

I'll tell you what else, sister! Saying no to the things that don't serve you allows you to say a big juicy *yes!* to opportunities that *are* absolutely going to light you up and be totally right for you. By turning down things that aren't in alignment with your values or that don't help you get ahead, you're creating space to be able to do the things *you* desire, to serve the people *you* want to help most.

Creating space enables you to spend time with the people *you* want to be spending time with. You're also allowed to say no to the things that don't allow you to grow, because *not* saying no basically stuffs your schedule with things you don't need or want.

I urge you to take a good, hard look at your calendar and tell me if all the events, meetings, and tasks in it are ones that you actually *want* to do—or even better, those you put there yourself, versus the ones that are there at the request of someone you couldn't say no to.

Step Two: Appreciate that you simply can't please everyone.

If you're one of those people pleasers who says yes because you just can't stand letting people down, you need to really dig deep and look at the actions as to why you do this.

If you're always saying yes and you think you're pleasing people, what you're really doing is becoming a pushover. Somebody who everybody can come to and go, 'Oh that Natalie, she always says yes to anything. I shove all my work onto her because she simply will never say, "No, bugger off. I've got too much work and you keep asking me to do stuff that is your responsibility"'.

So step back for a minute and think: While you're pleasing other people, are you actually losing respect for yourself and with others, because you simply cannot say no?

Step Three: Become more assertive.

If you simply can't stop saying yes to everything and consequently your life is chaotic, out of control, and you're miserably unhappy, you need to be more assertive.

So once again let's rehearse it. If it helps, try out the 'Blue Steel' approach of Ben Stiller's character in the movie *Zoolander*. Turn your head away from the person you're about to respond to, and as you snap it back to face them, put on a steely gaze, a strength of conviction, and even a pout if you wish—but no smiling—and simply say, 'No thanks'.

It takes courage, it takes confidence, and it takes practice. I totally get this.

The first time you try it, the other person may look shocked because they're so used to you saying yes. But don't turn around and say, 'Oh no, I didn't actually mean it, yes for sure I can'.

Take a breath instead, and let it sink in for them.

You become more assertive when you know what your why is, your fundamental reason for saying yes to the opportunities that you really want to take in the first place. This will allow you to be more assertive about saying no to the things that completely do not need to be on your to-do list and aren't relevant or important to you.

Step Four: Apologise less.

I actually have to catch myself out on this a lot, because I will say sorry even when it's not related to me or something I need to apologise for. Maybe it's from the two years I spent living in Canada, eh?

Somebody knocks into me in the street and I say, 'Oh sorry'. That's not something I need to apologise for! Or I will say something and then I'll just say sorry. The person I'm speaking with will stop me and say, 'Why are you sorry?' And I respond, 'I have no idea, sorry.' Then I catch myself and think no, no, no!

Stop with the damn apologising all the time, girl!

The good news is, there's this cool little phrase that works really well. If you apologise and you don't actually mean it, like it was an impulse or a reaction, immediately say, 'Sorry not sorry'. If you keep the sentence rolling you end up with 'Oh yeah, I'm sorry not sorry', and it actually gets you out of the habit of saying it when you don't need to.

Being less apologetic is a big part of being able to say no more because you're not saying sorry for saying no. You're simply saying no.

Start recognising when you're apologising for things or feeling guilty about saying no to things, and instead realise that it's a totally legitimate response to a request that you don't need to agree on. Got it?

Step Five: Learn to put you first more often.

The reason why I think so many of us say yes to things that we really don't want to do is that we're really, really good at giving. This is particularly important message for us women because we're really good at putting others first. So the people-pleasing behavior is actually saying, 'I'm not good enough to create some time and space for me, therefore I'm going to say yes to you, because clearly what you're doing is more important than my own awesome life'.

So it's really about putting *you* first and asking yourself:

- Does this align with what I want to do?

- Does this make me happier?

- Is this going to make my day more awesome?

- Is this going to make my life better?

- Am I going to feel like I'm contributing to something worthwhile?

- Am I going to become a better person as a result of saying yes to this?

If not, then it's a no thank you.

Step Six: Be happy with your decision.

As I said earlier, the minute you've said no, don't back up and go, 'Oh wait, I probably can, yeah okay, yeah all right. I'll squeeze it in'. If you have to, after saying no thank you, just smile and walk away. You don't have to say no and then back it up with an excuse, like 'I'm actually gonna be having my tonsils taken out that day and I just I just need a little bit of time because I won't be able to speak'.

You don't need to give an excuse. 'No, thank you' is perfectly adequate. Simply be happy with your decision, and then you can go hop around and think, 'Woohoo, I got out of doing that extra report', or 'I got out of that extra meeting', or 'I got out of this thing that I really didn't even want to volunteer for and now I don't have to do it. Now I have space and time to do the things I want to do and love doing with the people I love'.

It's a beautiful thing.

Step Seven: Let go of guilt.

You do not have to feel guilty for saying no, even if it's one of your best friends asking, 'Will you be a bridesmaid at my wedding?' Okay that's a pretty important question, but you can even say no to that. Granted you may want to give a bit more of a reason for this, but if your friend respects you and loves you, and you legitimately do not want to be her bridesmaid, it should stop there.

No guilt. If a person who requested something of you that you don't want to do is making you feel guilty, then 1) they're not a person you want to spend energy on, and 2) you actually have my permission to tell them to bugger off.

Unless it's a really bizarre scenario, everybody should be understanding. Sure hearing no is disappointing. Nobody likes rejection, but if it's done in a good way, then a 'no, thank you' followed by a smile is much easier to take. Even better is when you're able to talk to them about what they could do instead, who else they could ask, or how they could solve their own problem. You can still help them without actually having to be the person doing the thing. In that way, you've given them a valuable gift. It also makes you feel less guilty for saying no, even though you should feel no guilt!

Are we crystal clear?

The result of the seven steps I've laid out for you is that you instantly earn more respect. Think about a time you asked somebody to do something for you and they politely declined (whether by email, over the phone, or to your face) and your reaction was: 'Hmm that person's got her shit together'. Or 'They know their boundaries'. Or 'Wow, that's ballsy. I wish I could do more of that. How did they do that so easily?'

I love working with my entrepreneurial clients, who have finally said to their own clients:

- No I won't be available after 5:00 p.m.

- No you can't call me at 8:00 p.m. at night.

- No you can't call me when I'm on holiday.

- No, I don't offer discounts. That's the investment.

It instantly puts you at the forefront of their mind as somebody who has their shit together, knows their boundaries, and won't be messed with. That earns you kudos and respect, right?

That's what you want as an entrepreneur, a freelancer, as the master of your career, a mum, a sister, a girlfriend, a bestie, a community leader—and all the other roles you juggle in a given day. You want respect and the only way to earn that is to be very clear on what you will and won't say yes to and then to stay true to your boundaries, stay true to your word, and stay true to the integrity with which you approach everything.

Now you've learned the power of saying no, I want you to practice it:

1. Catch yourself in the next conversation you're having, where there's a request to do something you do not want to do.

2. Take a breath before saying: No, thank you.

3. Take another breath, pause, and wait for their response.

4. If their response is anything other than 'Oh, okay, fair enough'—follow up with 'I'd like you to respect my response of no. Can you do that for me?'

I think you'll be pleasantly surprised with the progress you make as you get better at it.

When you first try this out, tune into what feelings come up for you. Fear? Guilt? Shame? Or is it 'Oh my gosh, this person won't like me anymore'? Write that down. And next time you go to say no, I promise it'll be easier. Then the third time, it'll actually be delightful, and by the fourth time it'll be addictive!

Now, I'm not saying you need to say no to everything, just to the things that do not feel good, that do not align with your why, that do not serve a purpose, or that deter you from being the best possible version of yourself.

That's it; I'm done with the lecture. You are amazing. Yes, you are, and no, you don't have to go and do that thing that you don't want to do. You have the power to say no.

YOUR WORD IS EVERYTHING

Ever catch yourself speaking to yourself like you're an idiot? Or perhaps you're even harsher with a line like 'You stupid bitch, what on earth were you thinking?!'

Or perhaps you catch yourself complaining a lot, about anything and everything. 'Oh it's so rank that this restaurant doesn't have decent chairs. Why don't they invest in better ones? I'm so uncomfortable'.

'Why the heck are they taking so long to seat us? This is ridiculous'.

'Ah damn it, it's raining. This is going to suck now, because the event is outside'.

'Oh I have a foot pain. And my hip hurts.'

The trick is to catch yourself complaining, and to notice what you are complaining about all the time. Then say 'Okay, I'm gonna stop doing that', and when people ask you how you are, even if you have a headache, tell them you're great.

Why? Isn't it kind of fun to complain, rant, and moan from time to time? Not really. Does it *actually* make you feel better? In my experience, it makes me feel worse. That's because I realise I sound like an entitled Princess.

However, the real reason is that what you focus on expands. And you don't want to expand on more pain or negativity. Instead, you want to focus on how lucky you are to be alive, or that you're so glad you got a table at the restaurant with your dear friends you get to enjoy dinner with.

The other thing is to pay attention to your wording when you use extreme language such as always, won't, never, can't, and should. Those kinds of words indicate where your beliefs are focused. So it's important to pay attention to the language we use to describe things.

'I should go to the gym'. Really, why *should* you?

Be mindful of those words you're using. They help us understand where we're oriented, what drives us, and what's motivating us to take or not to take action.

Language is incredibly powerful. It's what we use to express what we believe. And that belief component is really the thing that ends up holding us back or propelling us forward.

We express our beliefs through our words.

We express our beliefs through our actions.

We express our beliefs through our relationships.

We express our beliefs through what we allow and don't allow, what works and doesn't work.

I'll give you an example. When I first started my online business, someone told me I should be speaking on stage about my blog turned business, and even make being a professional speaker part of my revenue streams.

My initial reaction was 'Oh, heck no, me a professional speaker? That's too big a leap for me to make. I mean I'm so new to this'. I didn't yet believe I was capable.

Strike forward a whole year and I was finally ready to step up and ask for more speaking gigs, even paid ones. That's because I had wrapped my head around the idea that actually I can get paid to speak, I can work on my skills and really make a go of it. I have a belief that I can do it, that I have valuable things to say and teach, whereas the year before I was nowhere near ready.

What this means is that your belief is the stopping place for whether or not you achieve your goals or dreams. Your belief is how you see yourself, how you describe yourself, and even how someone has described us for years and years that we have bought into believing.

For me, I'd always wanted to write a book since I was kid. Then in 2013, I felt I finally had something valuable to write about. I decided to state publically that I was writing my first book so that I wouldn't let myself or others down by not completing it. I mean, if I can't even keep my word to myself, well then my word is worth nothing.

In Steven Pressfield's *The War of Art: Break Through the Blocks and Win Your Inner Creative Battles*, I loved reading his recommendation that you call yourself an author when you're writing your first book, or any book. That simple yet important flip in his brain took him from screwing up every piece of paper he was writing on, to buying a typewriter, booking a cottage, and taking himself seriously enough to write his first book, not just saying 'Oh, I'm just writing a book'. He'd introduce him to others as an author, and now he got to live up to that description, because the more he said it, the more it became his belief.

Henry Ford said it best: "Whether you think you can, or you think you can't – you're right".

If you choose to believe you'll never do, be, or have what you want, that's exactly what will happen.

If you choose to believe that it's totally possible, then it's going to be totally possible.

It really is that simple. Start with what you want, and the 'how' to make it happen will come. At the end of the day, what we believe to be true about ourselves will promote us or prevent us from reaching our goals.

So why not talk about and visualise the best possible version of you!

CREATE YOUR IDEAL MORNING RITUAL

Does this sound like you?

Your alarm goes off and you wake up a little groggy. Immediately you grab your phone by your bed and start your swiping and scrolling ritual. You turn to Twitter, Facebook and Instagram to see your updates and notifications and attend to any 'urgent' business.

Before you know it over 30 minutes has gone by and you wonder where time goes! So you get up, get dressed in some form of workout gear with the best intentions to go after breakfast.

While making breakfast, you're checking your phone for any further updates, half texting, half stirring your porridge or your eggs, or sipping your coffee or tea. Likely you're unaware what the weather is doing outside and you're already engrossed in your workday.

If you work from home like me, you probably have your laptop open already while eating your breakfast, completely distracted by checking emails or your YouTube notifications, instead of simply being present and enjoying your cereal or eggs on toast.

Before you know it two hours have passed and you're still in your workout gear, still at that table and on your second or third cup of coffee and you haven't actually gotten to your to-do list for today.

LET'S CHECK IN WITH YOU. HOW ARE YOU FEELING RIGHT NOW?

A. Successful because you've been on the go all morning being busy

B. A little stressed because you've been up for hours already, but haven't got much done yet, if anything valuable

C. Frustrated because once again your dirty habits have worked against you

D. Fed up and wanting to know how to stop this time-sucking routine

I'm not a mind reader but I'd hazard a guess that it's likely B, C, or D.

Yes, I know where you're at because I still catch myself doing that from time to time, when I 'forget' to plug my phone in and leave it in my office, or out of reach.

Do you know what? It never works. Trust me. I never feel successful, energised, structured, and on top of the world when I let *anything* or *anyone* distract me from the moment I wake up, and pull me further away from my true purpose.

Why? Because you have not given yourself even the slightest bit of time to just *be*. To take stock of how your body feels this morning, whether your quality of sleep was good, what you're grateful for, what you feel in the mood for—sexy time, writing, strategy, marketing, exercise, reading, or perhaps even dancing!

You've mindlessly eaten your breakfast and plonked your ass in a chair for half a day and got more and more bogged down. Basically you've spent your entire waking moments not being present and not looking after yourself, and protecting your Queen before anything else.

So what should you be doing instead?

CREATE YOUR IDEAL MORNING RITUAL.

It starts with you determining what it's going to take to have an amazing day, kick ass, and feel like you've won the lottery.

Your morning ritual is unique to you. There are a bazillion blog posts, books, videos, and speeches out there on what you *should do,* but here's a thought: Why don't you do what *you want to do?*

You are the CEO of your own life, so start owning it.

If you want a few ideas, try looking at the habits of successful people. Choose the ones that speak to you to create your own unique daily ritual that will give you energy, focus, and a lot more time to do what you want.

I know you'd love an example or two, so first off I'll share mine, and then we'll explore some key habits and strategies that have worked for millions of others for centuries.

MY MORNING RITUAL

- Wake up naturally around 5:30am with the birds (or whenever I damn well feel like it)

- Do a big-ass delicious stretch in bed

- Feel extremely grateful to be alive and share my gratitudes with Josh

- Kiss and cuddle Josh (and maybe more depending on the mood!)

- Sip my warm herbal tea in a flask beside my bed and fully hydrate

- Do a meditation session sitting up in bed (or lying down cos I feel like it!)

- Kiss and cuddle Kayla and Angel (dog love is the *best*)

- Step into my yoga gear and head to my yoga room or jump in our electric car and head to my Crossfit class

- Sip on a cup of warm lemon water to cleanse and kickstart my digestive system

- Enjoy a delicious hot shower and when I want, finish off with 30 seconds of cold to enliven my body fully and get the blood pumping to deliver more oxygen to my body

- Head to my at-home office, turn on the essential oil diffuser, and open my LifePilot spreadsheet to check on my three most important actions for the day across my eight areas of life

- Dive into the most important priority to move the needle on my business (which may be a live coaching call, writing, team call, or strategic planning session)

· Enjoy a yummy green smoothie and scrummy breakfast after one hour of focused work.

It's entirely up to me to change this up, but I find the rhythm of it grounding and restorative. The absolute non-negotiable is moving my body first thing, and typically through yoga, Crossfit, or a run. Even just ten minutes makes me feel like a million dollars, and *everyone* can invest ten minutes to start their day off right.

So what do the people who 'have it all together' do?

After studying this for years, and implementing through trial and error, I've found a pretty solid 30 minute session you can adapt to suit you.

PHASE 1: MOVE AND BREATHE (10 MINUTES)

I don't care where you live, whether you're on the road for work, attending a conference that starts early, or taking a long commute. The first thing you do when you hear your alarm, or better yet wake naturally, is *leap* out of bed and move your body!

Yep, only 10 minutes. Examples are yoga, dancing, skipping, a brisk walk, or some simple body weight exercises, like press-ups and squats. Trust me, it will feel so good to get up and get some oxygen pumped into your lungs.

Hint: You'll probably find once you're out and exercising that you want to extend this into 20–30 minutes or even a run, a strength workout, a walk in the park, or a swim in the local pool. Whatever you enjoy or feel great after doing, do it.

PHASE 2: GET GRATEFUL AND VISUALISE (10 MINUTES)

Do you ever catch yourself saying, 'If only I had this, if only I could do this, I wish I was more this, this and this'? How about starting off your morning instead saying something like this, or writing it down:

> I am grateful for my great health, and the fact that I am able to do anything with my body—dance, sing, leap, swim, jump, run, dive, and push myself.

> I am grateful for Mother Nature surrounding me with the great outdoors, fresh air, beautiful trees and

flowers, amazing insects and animals that I get to experience every day.

I'm so happy I have a loving father/mother/partner/husband/wife/dog/cat/tiger in my life. They make my day and I love spending time with them. I am so blessed to have an awesome network of friends who make me laugh and smile.

I am honoured to have an incredible business partner/talented team/job I love to make me realise how far I can go in life.

I know today that I will be on fire, that I will rip through my to-do list and focus on the top 20% of tasks that will bring me 80% of the results.

I will attract amazing clients to my business or job who make my work easy through word-of-mouth referrals. I will develop a new system to work smarter, not harder. I will then maximise my opportunities by making incredible new contacts at the networking meeting tonight.

You get my point. How good does that make you feel just reading these ideas? You have also created your own reality by visualising how you want your day to look.

The mind has trouble distinguishing between something you vividly imagine and what you actually experience, so create what you want. Being grateful focuses you on how lucky you are and makes your own worries seem trivial in the scheme of things.

PHASE 3: INCANTATIONS OR MEDITATION (10 MINUTES)

Before I lose you completely as you imagine yourself chanting and dancing around a room, think about this. If you told yourself every morning that you were ugly, what would do that to your self-confidence? Now imagine you started your day with a daily meditation mantra that left you feeling on cloud nine, more abundant, giving, happy, or successful. Sounds fantastic to me.

It's also a great alternative if the idea of sitting quietly and attempting to observe your thoughts as a form of meditation makes you want to cry or run away.

Go for it, be big, be bold, and believe in yourself. Here are a few examples to use:

- Love is in everything. Love is everything.

- I belong. I feel. I am.

- Energy in. Energy out.

Or go for a beautiful mantra like *om mani padme hum*, which is used by Tibetan Buddhists to achieve the ultimate state of compassion.

Of course you can also make your own personal mantra. Here's how:

- Start with a word that means something to you, or that relates to your goal for your session, like joy, love, harmony, or peace.

- Give your mantra a direction and ground it in the positive, such as 'I am peaceful' or 'I am calm' (rather than 'I am worried').

- Repetition is the key here, especially if you're just beginning. Relax and start with saying your mantra up to 20 times, but don't count, just aim for a length of time.

- Speak it out loud. This engages your physiology and conditions the ideas into your mind.

- Use powerful words—none of this 'kind of, nice, possibly, maybe'.

The ultimate goal of a mantra is to block the world outside, so the more you repeat and concentrate on your mantra, the deeper you will dive inside your consciousness.

Gift yourself ten minutes to meditate. That's all you need to reduce stress, decrease anxiety, improve your cardiovascular health, and achieve a greater capacity for relaxation. Not sure you can spare the time? Come on, you're worth it. Do this for a week, and if you don't see results then call me a liar.

If you can't take out 30 minutes for yourself in the morning, then either get up earlier than the rest of the household, or break it up into three 10-minute sessions throughout the day. I can guarantee that by the end of the week you'll achieved more than you thought possible, and that you did it with energy, focus, and conviction.

Even better, you'll discover that you reclaimed more time in your day because you'd got the important stuff out of the way, and you feel more grounded and peaceful too.

SHOW UP AND YOU'RE 90% THERE

I've played sports all my life. I love trying new things, the competitiveness of it, pushing myself, and the team camaraderie.

In 2004, I decided to switch to training for triathlons to find out what an individual pursuit was like, what my body was capable of doing, and how I could transform it. I hired a personal trainer to help me because I really had no clue about triathlons and how to train for them.

The trainer looked amazing. She was strong. She was lean. She was muscular and yet still feminine. I had never seen a physique like it. Curious, I asked her what she was training for and she said body sculpting competition.

'A body sculpting what?' I replied.

I looked it up and I immediately thought, what a bizarre sport. You basically get really lean. You work out a heap. You massively restrict your diet so you're eating 'clean'.

You put on a lot of muscle. And then you stand up on stage with this ridiculous bronze tan on you and strike some poses in a skimpy bikini.

Despite that, something about it really intrigued me, because in all my years of playing sport I had never changed my body shape. I'd always pretty much look the same. I was so impressed and fascinated by this lady that I wondered, what would it take to change my body and do something completely different?

I asked her about the competitions she'd entered, and she admitted that she hadn't been able to sacrifice sugar, and so all her hard work and dedication had gone nowhere and she wound up choosing not to compete. I thought it was really sad to put in all that effort and then not take it further because you couldn't give up sugar for a few months.

I asked her a load more questions, went home, googled upcoming competitions, and decided to go for it. I chose one that was nine months out, because I thought that was enough time to get in shape.

I didn't end up hiring a trainer but I did hire the nutritionist at my favourite gym, Les Mills. He not only gave me a nutrition plan, but also a weights workout to help me as he worked with all the local bodybuilders and body sculptors.

Within weeks I was slowly stripping out all the fun stuff in life—the unhealthy burgers, chips, pizzas, and Chinese takeaways that I was very fond of. I viewed it as a nine-month period of eating really clean and healthy, going to the gym seven times a week, and working out really hard for an end goal—competing in my first novice 'figure', aka body sculpting, competition.

Three months in, my boyfriend at the time told me he was really proud of me, doing all this training and eating clean, but deep down he didn't think I would stick with it.

'Why's that?' I asked, a little hurt and perplexed.

'Well, you just don't stick with things for very long and you like to do new things all the time'.

He hadn't meant it in a bad way; he believed he was just being honest. I thought he had a point too, until I looked at all the things I had been doing for years in my life, and had stuck with. Like playing tennis, netball, studying, travelling, working, and playing piano.

His comment stayed in my head, and frankly pissed me off. I used it as ammunition to continue on, because between you and me, I was already starting to doubt whether this was a good idea. I'd sacrificed a lot already and wasn't seeing any major results. But as with all things worth doing in life, good things take time. And a few weeks later I started seeing the results of my hard work and discipline.

A defined triceps muscle here, a little visible ab here, a bicep that was bigger than a few centimetres there. It got me encouraged. I kept at it. Around this same time I started visualising.

It was a tool I'd learned through being in sports teams, and also back in a job I had in London where I talked my way into attending a speaker training event in the Tuscan countryside of Italy (as one does!). I remembered how effective it had been for talks and presentations I'd done since then, and how it helped me prepare so that on the day I felt ready and performed at my best.

I used this handy tool to visualise being up on stage, doing my routines and poses, and winning the division! Every single morning when I went to the gym, I took a small booklet with my workout routine in it, the weights and exercises I had to do, so I could track what I was lifting. I used it in a very disciplined way, and filled that out every single time, seven times a week, sometimes twice a day.

At the top of that piece of paper in this booklet I had written: *Countdown to comp win.*

Basically, somewhere in my head, I decided that I was going to win the competition. And so I wrote it on that piece of paper and that's the same piece of paper I looked at seven days in a row for close to nine months.

Strike forward to October of 2004 and I'm standing on the stage in Hamilton, New Zealand, at the regional Body Sculpting Championships. I'm in the Novice Tall Figure category. Body sculpting is also called 'figure', because you're not big and muscular. You're actually quite lean and feminine, although I did have an eight pack and an awesome arse, with amazing and pert muscles, which are never going to be like that again, but it was pretty impressive looking back at the photos.

Anyway I digress. I'm standing on stage in these sexy heels that I actually had to buy at a stripper shop. I've got way too much bronze fake tan on. I'm in a tiny little blue spangly bikini and I'm posing and showing off my abs, my biceps, my triceps, and my lats in the ways I'd been taught by a trainer who specialised in holding these poses. Showing off your muscles and physique while holding these poses in a pair of heels you can barely walk in, under bright shining lights, is way harder than I anticipated. Then it was on to the routine to music, where you have to strike a number of these poses in around two minutes or less.

I had got the help of a dance choreographer friend to make my routine outstanding. I chose 'What a Feeling' from the *Flashdance* soundtrack, and nailed it! The crowd loved it; up until then most of the routines were monotonous and repetitive. But I had myself start in a crouch, went into a fancy roll, and even a cartwheel— because why the heck not!

After we'd all had our turn on stage, they started calling out names of people who were going to make it into the judging round and I realised, in that very moment, that I had not even entertained the thought of not winning. All I thought about in the back of my mind was winning. I'd simply focused on the result I'd wanted from early on in order to get to this point. And here I was on the stage and they were calling out who they were going to take forward and all I could think was, 'Shit, I haven't prepared not to win. How am I going to deal with this if I don't make it?

Luckily, a few moments later I was called forward too, which was awesome. Now I was standing in the glaring lights, with two other ladies, each of us tensing in our poses to look our best, teetering on these damn heels, smiling without a break...waiting, and waiting.

Then came the announcement: "In third place, for the Novice Tall Figure competition..." they called out someone's name. She came forward, happy to accept her gift and little trophy. "The runner up for the Novice Tall Figure competition..." and they called someone else's name.

This is it, I thought to myself, the moment I've been waiting for. I glanced at the lady to my left (I had ended up in the middle), and I thought, nah I got this. She looks great, but damn I worked my ass off for this—literally and figuratively, plus I have no idea what I'll do if they don't call my name.

I could feel myself getting a little emotional, and hungry, always hungry when you're eating mainly chicken and broccoli, day in, day out , but constantly in calorie deficit for me to stay at 10% bodyfat.

The announcer paused for dramatic effect. It felt like eternity. Then he called out the name.

"And the winner is Natalie Sisson, from Wellington."

I *beamed*!

I'd won, holy crap, I'd won.

I stepped forward, relieved. He shook my hand, said some congratulatory words, handed me a huge tub of protein powder, a skimpy workout top, and the biggest, tackiest, gold and green trophy I'd ever seen.

I was so proud. I also found out I'd made it into the National finals happening two weeks later. Whaaaat?

Once off stage, I ran out to see my parents and my boyfriend, who were all so thrilled for me. Then Mum announced matter-of-factly, 'Can we go home now, Nat? I don't think I can handle seeing one more orange bronzed body come on stage, pose so stiffly, and look so serious!'

Yep, we sure can. Oh, and I'd like to eat a burger!

ATTRACT WHAT YOU DESIRE

I admit it, I became a fan of the Netflix show *Lucifer* for a short time. It's got all the right ingredients for lighthearted fun and hilarious entertainment, combined with good-looking people and some cracking one-liners.

And who can resist the devilishly handsome Lucifer (see what I did there), who can look into your eyes and ask, 'What is it that you truly desire?' and everyone tells him the truth.

My question to you is, how often do you actually ask yourself the same question, and answer it honestly?

You might even be able to pinpoint times that you've really, truly wanted something, put time and attention into it, dreamed about it even, and then days, weeks, or even months later it came true.

What causes that? Is it the law of attraction? Perhaps you've seen or read *The Secret,* which explains how the law of attraction works. Maybe you're big time into manifesting? Perhaps quantum physics is your jam?

In my humble opinion, use whatever works, baby—whatever it takes to get you to where you want to be, and who you want to be. I'm more into the law of action: As in take action and shit gets done. Things happen. Take consistent, repetitive action on the right things, and your life will become pretty freaking amazing.

In case you need a refresher or simply have no idea what the heck I'm going on about, the law of attraction is an idea that through cosmic law or quantum physics, whatever you focus on expands. So rather than focusing on negative thoughts, you want to focus instead on what you want more of.

Like attracts like. So if you constantly focus your thoughts on what you want to manifest, you will attract those things. As a result, you'll attract other people whose thoughts are resonating at the same frequency and before you know it, you're having a wild manifestation orgy!

It's actually a lot simpler than that. People act when they believe their actions will be rewarded and their goals will be reached. Without that belief in potential success, you take no action, and without action there's no outcome or accomplishment.

It all starts with our beliefs. Our beliefs control our thoughts. Our thoughts create our actions, and our actions impact our results. So if you believe something is possible, it's much more likely to happen, and repetition fuels belief.

Repeatedly visualising a deeply sought-after goal, seeing, feeling, smelling, and hearing yourself accomplish this goal over and over has a profound effect. It conditions you slowly away from self-doubt and disbelief and moves you increasingly toward belief.

The beautiful thing is that the more you believe, the more likely you are to act. When you truly believe something even marginally you begin to do a thousand little things differently.

- You dress better.

- You talk to people who've intimidated you in the past.

- You ask better questions, and get better answers.

- You become more confident.

- You hang out with accomplished people.

- You invest time, energy, and money in yourself and others.

You are actually showing up differently, although you may not notice it, yet all these tiny or seemingly insignificant changes impact your life in profound ways.

People you interact with see these changes being made in your life. They perceive you differently, they become more responsive to you, because you seem more attractive to them, because of your increased confidence, commitment, and energy. All those little consistent actions you've been taking start to add up and have a big effect on your life. Gradually, they will bring you closer to your goals.

The thing is, each of those small actions probably seems insignificant in and of itself, and the results that you start to get seem like they're coming out of nowhere, almost like magic! Each positive interaction simply fuels your belief that was initially set in motion by your original conditioning or thought, and this sets in motion a belief, action, and attainment cycle that gradually grows in force.

Simple, yet powerful, right?!

Repeatedly visualising a goal as if you had already attained it conditions you to believe it's possible over time as that conditioning takes root through repetition. Just look at my body sculpting example in the previous chapter for proof!

Your belief in success leads you to act differently on so many levels and take actions you wouldn't have otherwise taken. I see it all the time in my clients. They make small shifts in the way they're thinking, or what they tell themselves, coupled with what I'm teaching and coaching them on, and then they act on those, consistently.

Like Emma, one of my Queens in the $10K Club, who continues to inspire me through her willingness to do the work and go all in. The leaps and bounds she made in just a few short months were magical:

#win Just when I was about to start doubting this new offering I'm doing, I had a woman register and pay in full for a full year of the VIP package that includes 1:1 coaching at my new higher prices! And this little boost just put me at almost double the revenue goal I set for June! I think maybe I'm finally done with the doubt now. I'm prepared to laugh in its face if it tries to creep up again!

Or Helen, who wrote:

#win Hey lovely people, I wanted to share a thing that happened....

I got clear with my vision and wrote out my goals in the life canvas...and then, in keeping with my goals, today I launched a new, flagship course that is totally aligned with what I really want to offer.

With just one post on LinkedIn I've had four applications. (I want five people to sign up and I've got one other person in the wings, who's super keen.) HOLY MOLY!

Not really sure what I'm doing now/next/at all...but it's out there and it's a new revenue stream and I made it happen.

DAMN THAT'S FAST!

Totally scared. But stepping into it and ignoring all the fear!

In another post she even commented, 'Who am I?!' She was actually surprised at who she was becoming, through her new beliefs and aligned actions.

Those actions increasingly deliver results and inspire you to believe your vision is attainable on a deeper level, which inspires even more action. As people around you see you not only succeeding, but becoming more confident and passionate, they respond to that confidence.

Pretty logical, really—no need to read *The Secret.* It's all about a commitment to action; you can't manifest something out of thin air. You have to show up, and commit to action.

BE INTENTIONAL

I love me some goal setting. Heck I can attribute most of my success in life and business to aligning my goals with my big-picture dreams, and then going after them with determination. But they're not the be-all and the end-all, and goals alone won't get you to the results you desire. In short, goals are focused on the future. They're about a destination or a specific achievement and goals.

If I didn't have goals in place to compete in my first ever Half Ironman (Ironwoman), I probably never would have gotten a training plan together to build up my endurance over the months through runs, bike rides, and swim sessions. I most certainly wouldn't have been fit and ready for the event if my goal hadn't been to do well and also enjoy it. And I definitely wouldn't have gotten up early in the morning to train.

Goals have an absolute benefit. They drive you. They give you a focus. They give you a deadline, a timeline. They give you something that you can aim for and achieve, and they give you purpose. And so they're brilliant when they're about a future event. You can set up your strategies for it. You can prepare, plan, and really know what you're going for.

Want to know what's more powerful? Intentions.

Intentions are in the present moment.

Intentions are lived each day independent of reaching the goal or destination.

You have probably felt this before, when you've set yourself a big juicy goal and then let's say maybe you've hit it, but once you've achieved it or smashed it you have this sense of disappointment or deflation afterward.

The big lesson to learn there is that you also have to have an intention of how you're going to show up every single day. It's not just about that one goal. Hopefully, your intention is to be the best version of yourself, to live with passion, to be on purpose, to be kind, to be generous, to be driven, to be ambitious, or whatever else your desire is.

How you want to show up in this world is *the* thing that you need to put all your energy and effort into. It's what you're going to focus on every single day. It's how you are going to live and breathe and act with that intent.

When you have intentions that are backed up by these goals and milestones, you're not going to get depressed or disappointed or upset after something, because that goal won't be the be-all and the end-all of how you live.

It's just the next driver. It's the next point that you're trying to reach, but because your intentions are constantly with you, those are the things that are always going to carry you through. Goals are needed, but intentions are what is going to help you show up in this world, and they're going to be with you long after you've hit and smashed all your goals that I know you're going to do.

Now it's your turn. Within the next 30 days, what is one goal and one intention you want to set for yourself?

SET AND SMASH YOUR OWN RECORDS

After ten months of training at 6.30 a.m. on the River Thames and weekends on the South England coast, the day had finally arrived.

It was a gorgeous, sunny, and relatively still Saturday on the 25th of August 2007, and we, the Sisterhood, were ready for the adventure that lay ahead.

Picture eighteen of us fantastic women paddlers and one helm, about to set an unofficial world record as the fastest and first ever all-female crew to dragon boat across the English Channel. Our aim was to smash the current world record time.

I had volunteered to be in charge of making sure that happened. I'd contacted Guinness World Records, received the paperwork, and shared the key details of what was necessary to satisfy their criteria with Emma Sayle and Debra Searle, the two powerhouses who'd made this entire thing possible.

We had to have a support boat, an official timekeeper, and someone to make sure we were doing it all properly. That job fell to our coach, Cam. Our coach had accounted for the combination of all four strengths needed in a dragon boat—physical, mental, attitudinal, and behavioral—as well as the ideal distribution of paddling abilities.

We had our 'peppy' front quad, who kept our pace and spirits high. I was in the physically and mentally strong middle, and then we had an attitudinally strong back-back. Every single thing had been meticulously planned, right down to what snacks and water we could take on board with us and our combined weight as a crew.

The time came for us to start our 21.1-mile journey from Shakespeare's Beach in England to Wissant Bay in France, which included crossing the world's busiest shipping lane.

We did it and it was epic. We absolutely smashed the world record time. The previous record had been set at around 7 hours. We did it in 3 hours and 42 minutes. We were also only 12 minutes behind the Brotherhood—the team with which we had a healthy rivalry!

We fell out of the boat when we got to France, and drank the champagne handed to us by our friends and family who'd come on the support boat.

We rolled around in the shallow waves by the shore, hugging, laughing, and sharing stories from our own accounts of the crossing. I honestly think this was one of the biggest highs I've experienced in my lifetime (helped by the effect of the champagne, I'm sure).

Once we'd all partied with the Brotherhood and landed back in London, I set about submitting the videos, photos, timekeeping, and records to the officials at Guinness.

About a week later we got a letter to inform us that we weren't awarded the official Guinness World Record for this. Even though we had smashed it, I found out that— to make it official—we should have had a dragon head and tail and somebody beating a drum on the dragon boat while we were crossing, because that's how people usually race.

If you've never witnessed a dragon boat in action, here's some context. The boat is around 12m long with sides only 20cm high, and the boats are very low to the water. Typically these boats are reserved for short 1,000m sprints in a safe lake or close to the ocean shore. They have a fancy and colourful dragon-style head out front and a tail sticking off the back—both extending out around a meter—and they weigh a lot!

You start with your paddle high up and then you plunge that paddle down to the water and pull back with a short, sharp stroke. The whole team has to be in synchronicity to make it go forward and go at pace. We managed to do this for nearly 4 hours over more than 20 miles! If we'd had a head and a tail and a drummer, we would have pretty much drowned.

Visualise a tiny boat crossing the English Channel— much vaster than the small bodies of water dragon boats generally navigate. We were but a blip on the ocean in the wake of some decent-sized waves made by the many container ships moving around us at about 40km an hour. We had to bust out carefully timed power paddle sessions to get our boat up to speed and well out of the way, before they got anywhere near us.

So yeah, a dragon head and tail made no sense, and was not even safe.

We were all super disappointed when we found out. That said, the lesson we learned from all this was that we still smashed that world record. We can still claim that internally, personally, and as a team. We were immensely proud of what we did.

What's more, we realised we didn't actually need the official record to be proud of ourselves. We had already congratulated and celebrated ourselves on that massive accomplishment. And we raised over £100,000 pounds for charity!

So what goal have you smashed recently that you're proud of? What ways are you celebrating all the things you are amazing at, or even the small things you've done?

You are the only one you need to prove yourself to. Deep down, you know you are already enough, and anything else is just icing on the cake.

PART 3

BECOME A WARRIOR PRINCESS

Traditionally, the term 'Princess' has been associated with entitlement and privilege, whereas a 'Warrior Princess' fights for what she wants to see in the world, and advocates for what is right, just, fair, and equitable. So that's the persona we are taking on today, as we rise up onto the saddle of our mighty horse, looking sexy and powerful in our functional armour, and fearlessly ride out to lead the way for ourselves and all women.

CERTAINTY IS YOUR SUPERPOWER

I thought I'd found my dream job back in early 2004, when I was a fresh-faced, keen bean wanting to work her way up in the corporate world. I'd just gotten back from travelling the world, and moved to Auckland with my boyfriend to start afresh in the big city.

I'd built up around two years' worth of marketing skills in various roles and was ready for the next big leap. I remember seeing a job listed by a recruitment agency that screamed at me, 'Natalie, this is perfect for you!' So I fired off my CV and sent a great cover letter, certain I'd get a response.

And I did. Except not the one I so wished for. It simply said:

Hello Miss Sisson,

Thank you for your application for the role of Brand Manager, Schwarzkopf Professional.

Unfortunately, there were more qualified candi-dates for the role, so we won't be taking your application further.

Thank you, and best of luck.

[Insert numbwit name here]

I was flabbergasted, because in my heart, body, and soul, I had already accepted this job offer. I just knew it was meant for me. Sure, my previous role was as a marketing assistant and this was a big step up. And yes, I had a few gaps on my resume due to taking time off to travel the world each time I got bored in a job and quit. Yes, there were a lot of things in the job description for which I had no experience.

But did they not know how awesome I was?

Clearly not. My overrated confidence in my abilities was at an all-time high. So, undeterred, I took the next logical step.

I rang the recruitment agent to tell them they had got it wrong.

From memory, that's pretty much what I did say, except in a much more eloquent way, that went something like this:

Hi X. My name's Natalie Sisson, and I recently received an email from you about the brand manager role at Schwarzkopf Professional.

'Oh yes'.

'Yes, you see the thing is you said I wasn't a fit for the role, but I believe I am, and I'd like the chance to prove it to you'.

'Oh...well, we've had a lot of interest in that role and some great applicants who are more qualified.'

'Yes I'm sure you have, but I'd like to meet with you to share why I think I'd be a great fit for this company and that I can 100% handle this role'.

'Hmmm well—'

'I can come in tomorrow if you have time and talk you through my experience and why I think I'm the right fit for this position. Please say yes'.

'Look, okay, let's do that, because to be honest this role is very much about finding the right personality fit with the management team, and so far that's not happened.'

And the rest, as they say, is history.

I nailed the in-person meeting and we got on like a house on fire, because she was a talented recruitment agent who was more invested in the right fit versus a resume that ticked some boxes. She rang the general manager while I was with her and said she'd like for him to see one more person she thought was a great fit, and to overlook my current work experience and just trust her on it.

He agreed and a few days later I met up with Craig, the GM, and we had a blast in the interview. I went back a few days later to meet a few more of the team, do some tests, and then *boom*!

I got my dream job. I even got a fancy fringe cut (bangs) in time for my first day on the job, and will never forget walking into the first sales team meeting with *all* eyes on me. I was attempting to sound like I knew what I was talking about when introducing the new product line of colour, and couldn't figure out why *everyone* was looking at me so intently.

I later found out that most of the sales team were ex-hairdressers and they couldn't wait to get their hands on me and give me a proper style and colour and get rid of my terrible fringe, or the sun-in I'd been using to bleach my hair!

I spent almost two extremely happy years in that job, with a great team and an extremely challenging position that I jumped in the deep end for. I ended up having a blast and being promoted to national brand manager—with at least ten different hairstyles during my time there.

I was most proud of creating a whole lot of awesome product launches, hair award shows, and marketing promotions that other countries' offices ended up modelling.

The key takeaway: never let a blanket rejection stop you from making your dreams come true. Back yourself. Be confident. Be certain. Choose *you*. And your dream may just land in your lap!

PUT YOURSELF OUT THERE

I was on a coaching call with my students in my Launch Your Damn Course Accelerator. A gorgeous lady from Ireland asked me, 'Natalie, how do I put myself out there?' This wasn't the first time I'd been asked that, and it won't be the last.

'How do you overcome that, Natalie? I've been following you for a long time, and I really admire you. You just put yourself out there, you know, and it's very admirable. So how do you do that?'

A few people echoed this in the chat on our Zoom call. I was humbled. Then I saw several people mention that they never see me selling.

This blew my mind! I shared with them that I'm almost always selling. I'm always excited about something, even if it's not my own creation, and I naturally share that enthusiasm with others in a way that gets them excited or on board with what I'm talking about or promoting. I use the power of inviting people and their curiosity, not pushing or cajoling them into doing or buying something they might have no interest in.

I thanked her for her kind words, and in true coaching style, I put the question back to her and asked, 'Of all the things that you've seen me putting myself out there about, what has made it engaging or useful to you versus salesy or over the top?'

For example, if I see somebody doing something really well, I ask:

- What was it that they did that I liked?

- Why was it engaging?

- Why did I click through to find out more?

I'm curious, is there anything that comes to mind?

Siobhain was instantly able to pinpoint what it was. 'That's so easy to answer, because you share your personal stories and always have and that is so engaging. You're very open. I'm a very open person and that resonates with me. Also your content is just super valuable, and not salesy. I recently unsubscribed from someone because they were bombarding me with so many sales emails I felt like they were going to turn up at my front door! So I suppose it's due to those two things: the value that you uphold and have always delivered, and your personality and that you're not afraid to show who you are'.

There you go—the answer to not selling is to just be yourself!

In answering that question for herself, she was able to learn what it was that worked for her, and how she could use her own unique style and personality to market herself and her course, in a way that felt great to her and to others.

Over the years, I've learned that you can be vulnerable and transparent, without giving away your entire world and privacy, and that makes you more relatable, likeable, and trustworthy.

For example, people might know about my beautiful dogs, Kayla and Angel. They might know about Josh, our travels, or see snippets of our house as I share interior design upgrades on Instagram or film videos on our land. But they don't know *all* the things going on in my life. In fact, there's a big portion of areas I'm interested in that I never talk about. I don't need to share that.

I share what is relevant that makes me more real—the struggles, the good things, and the not so good things. I don't think it detracts from what you're doing. If anything, it makes you more human and more relatable.

There have definitely been times in my career and business where I feel I've gotten to a certain point that makes me think, 'Wait a minute, am I coming across as that kind of expert where nobody can actually relate to me anymore?'

The answer was often 'You're pretty damn close, lady, so take a step back to earth!'

I've personally followed people I admired until they seem to have gotten so big for their boots and stepped so far out of alignment with their values that I can't even relate to them anymore. I don't want an eight-figure business, and I don't care about your private helicopter. Let's get back to those cool life lessons you teach so well.

In her early days, entrepreneur Marie Forleo used to sit on a couch in her apartment and just film a video on her mobile, speaking directly to it: 'Hey, it's Marie here'. She'd have a coffee cup in her hand, little makeup, tousled hair, ripped jeans, and a casual top. It was like real talk with your best friend.

Then she continued to expand and soon it became MarieTV and she had a production team, a set, a wardrobe specialist, a makeup artist, and big-name fancy guests. I totally understand that she needed to grow and evolve.

She had a goal and dream to be more like Oprah and she's a star in her own right now. But I actually preferred those videos from her early days because they were really real, and they were relatable. I'm not saying that you can't evolve and become more professional. Just don't lose sight of what makes you real, likeable, and trustworthy.

Share your professional opinion, experience, and skills. And also share the journey you're on too, and your real life. You can absolutely have an eight-figure business and still be yourself.

Whether you're homeschooling, going into plant-based eating, or getting out of debt, come at it from the point of view of 'Hey, this is what I'm learning and if it's valuable to you, come join me on my journey'. If you're passionate about it, and especially if you tell the story behind why this is important to you, people will buy into that. They'll come with you and they'll grow with you too. That's invaluable.

I have people who have listened to my podcast since 2012, who have been on my email list for a decade. And a special handful of people who've bought *everything* I've ever created. It stuns me, but damn I appreciate it. They're superfans. It doesn't matter if they don't even need it, they just want to support me and they appreciate what I put out in the world. (Special shoutout here to Saeema Salim; you're one of a kind, lady!)

That's why I really encourage you to start engaging and talking. Start getting more comfortable with putting yourself out there. Speak on topics you are curious about, that you have some knowledge about, or an opinion on. And share.

I've definitely had moments where I've thought about self-censoring, wondering, 'Oh, do I want to say this?' Then I do a reality check and think well, it's truthful, and it's from the heart, and it feels right in my gut, so I will share, especially if there's a lesson in it for somebody else.

I've talked to plenty of people who go to put themselves out there, put out an offer, or start a new project, and then they freeze up, because they don't want to come across as too salesy. They talk themselves out of turning up and being them.

The reality is that your first Facebook live will have zero to one viewers anyway, so if you feel like a right tool, who freaking cares? Hit the 'Go Live' button. Trust me—it gets easier over time, and everybody starts somewhere.

Simply share with enthusiasm. Be genuine. Tell your story. Share your why and most of all make it valuable to them. All of these factors combined are really compelling and people will love you for it. The ones who don't are not your people anyway.

The thing is, you need to love you too. You need to quit putting on a facade and be the real deal, quirks and all. That's when you'll step into your full power, Princess!

ASK FOR WHAT YOU WANT

Asking for what you want seems like a simple thing to do, doesn't it? Except I realised that most people I meet don't exercise this right every day. Requests like:

- Can I have an extra hot chai latte?

- Could you heat this soup up?

- Can I bring my booking forward?

These seem quite straightforward and doable, yet I know friends who will sit quietly and complain that their meal is cold or they didn't get what they ordered, rather than simply asking for what they want.

Whether it's out of some moral obligation not to be a 'bother' or it gets put in the too-hard basket, I'm not sure why more of us don't ask for what we want. Every time I ask them why they don't just ask for what they *really* want, I get a different answer. Most of them sound like excuses born from either laziness, entitlement, or a fear of rejection.

When you start getting into territory as follows, people start to get really freaked out:

- I'd like a pay rise of $X. Why? Because I'm worth it, and here's proof....

- I'd like to extend my contract, yes. And I'd like a company car along with that.

- My speaking fee is $10,000, not $5,000. If you can meet that, then yes, book me in.

- Can you introduce me to the CEO of X company in person so I can discuss a deal with her?

- I am happy to talk to that publisher if they will give me a six-figure advance on my book.

I personally *love* asking for exactly what I want, and it's brought me so many amazing opportunities in my life. One of my favourite mottos is: *Don't ask, don't get.*

Sure I might be cheeky, or pushing my luck, but why the heck not. What have I got to lose? What have you got to lose?

I never demand anything. I always ask with a smile and in a friendly manner. I don't ask for miracles. And this one is key: I already expect the answer to be yes, because I'm so certain it's an ask that can be granted.

Does this work every time? Heck no. But it works *most* of the time.

There's a lot to be said for being confident in your ask, and certain. Call it manifesting, call it law of attraction, or call it as it really is—belief in your thoughts, which become actions.

A really easy example in action is the fact that I'm the queen of parking. Josh officially calls me that all the time. He initially used to say, 'It's uncanny. How is there always a carpark free in the perfect place when you're driving?' Now he says, 'Okay, Parking Queen, work your magic'.

I'd say my hit rate is 98%. I just know there's going to be a carpark right outside the restaurant, or theatre, or the event we're going to. Is it because I asked the universe in advance, and it said, sure here you go, milady. Or is it that I don't entertain the thought of *not* getting the perfect carpark? You be the judge.

I've experienced this a lot on my adventures around the world too. Like the time our family were heading to Noosa, on the Sunshine Coast of Australia. That trip is one for the memory books.

We got to the airport, and Dad asked if there was any chance we could get an upgrade on the flight. The kind lady at the checkout asked if it was for all four of us, and we all smiled back with a look of 'but of course!'

'Actually, I can give you an upgrade to business class for all four of you in the same row. How does that sound?'

Sounded damn good to us. When we landed, I went with Dad to get the rental car we'd booked, while Mum and my sister went to get the bags. Before we got to the counter, I said to Dad, 'Hey, maybe we'll get an upgrade on the car too', knowing full well he'd probably booked the cheapest one!

As luck would have it, the person behind the counter said, 'Ah, Mr Sisson. I'm sorry but we don't have your car available. So we've upgraded you to a premium executive car. I hope that's okay'.

'Yes. It sure is!' we both replied, grinning.

Once the car was loaded, we drove off to the apartment we'd booked for a full week of school holiday goodness and when we got to the reception, it happened again!

'Welcome Mr and Mrs Sisson. We're so thrilled you're here to stay with us. We regret to inform you that your room isn't ready yet, but what we have done instead is upgraded you to the penthouse apartment. I trust that's ok with you?'

Damn right it is! And thank you, universe. We went on to have the best holiday ever. Particularly because with all those upgrades, Dad splurged a little more than normal on dinners out.

Probably one of my favourite examples of a 'Don't ask, don't get' moment was meeting Seth Godin.

Back in April 2010, I'd written a post called 'Feel the Fear. Follow Your Passion. Be a Linchpin.' I remember being stunned when Seth Godin himself, author of *Linchpin: Are You Indispensable?* left a comment on my blog: 'Well done! This is just the beginning. Can't wait to see what happens.'

As a fairly new blogger at the time, the fact that someone like Seth, who'd already written thousands of blog posts (he writes daily on his own) and around 18 bestselling books, blew me away.

I decided to email him, as I'd heard from a friend that he actually answered his emails. So around six months later I wrote:

> Loved the latest post Seth. I just wanted to drop you a line because I'm also reading Chris Guillebeau's book right now with your lovely testimonial and spoke with him this morning—always brings a smile to my day. Plus I just wrote a post (link below) that is all about freedom and living your own life.
>
> Anyhoo, I'm a tad closer to you (location wise) now I've left Canada to embark on my next adventure to Buenos Aires. A little too far from NYC to throw a Frisbee disc but I do intend to visit next year and will throw one at your house or office to get your attention and take you out for high tea.
>
> I still appreciate you taking time to comment on my blog when I wrote my 'Feel the Fear. Follow Your Passion. Be a Linchpin' post in April. You're the best— really.
>
> Hope you're extraordinarily well!

He simply replied, 'Happy Thanksgiving'. But I had planted the seed! I kept in touch with an email here and there.

When writing this chapter for *Suck It Up, Princess*, I searched my Gmail inbox to find an email conversation with a blogger from 2012, who'd asked to share my story on his blog. In my reply I said, 'Love that you interviewed Seth Godin—love your honesty in the interview too. Man, I'm jealous. I hope to MEET him when I'm in NYC—I'm going to make it happen.'

See what I did there. Certainty. Confidence. Believing it to be true.

Then in April 2012 I wrote an email to my community to celebrate my birthday, because I love birthdays. I shared my short birthday video on why Seth Godin has been a big influence on me personally over the years, and on my blog.

During the video I decided I'd give away seven copies of his new book *The Icarus Deception* to celebrate my blog's birthday. Social Media Today picked it up and published my blog in full, complete with my silly birthday photo.

To top it off, Seth Godin loved the video too and commented on my Facebook picture I took with his books. Pretty cool, really.

Fast forward to July 2013 and I'm getting ready to launch my first book and have sent out a campaign update to all of my wonderful pledgers on Kickstarter. The first line reads, 'I am soooooo excited to say that from today onward you'll start receiving—before anyone else (bar Seth Godin), a copy of my Suitcase Entrepreneur digital book'.

As you can see, I so admire the man that it's probably a slight obsession. But only in looking back on this did it become clear that I focused on what I wanted and continued to work toward it, even if no direct action was being taken.

I was not so secretly wanting him to write a blurb for my book—a very long shot, I know. But on September 9, 2013, I asked him via email:

> On the off chance you might be coming into Manhattan I'd love to say a quick hello and personally give you a paperback copy of my book that I have just a few copies of (not great for a Suitcase Entrepreneur to carry many around).
>
> PS It's a No #1 Bestseller on Amazon so I'm pretty thrilled; more importantly it's changing people's lives according to them.
>
> Hope you're super well.

His response:

> congratulations!
>
> alas, swamped, sorry
>
> enjoy the city

That was it. I replied, saying, 'How about I come out to yours. When suits?'

The nerve! Well that nerve worked. His response was 'Well if you want to make the schlep out to Hudson, sure let's do Wednesday at 2 p.m. Here's the address.'

OMG! This was really happening.

I took a train, bringing along a signed copy of my book. I got all flustered and nervous before ringing the intercom. No one answered for ages. Just as I wondered if I had taken this trip for nothing, he answered, 'Come on up'.

I spent a precious hour of time with Seth Godin, who made me tea and served me cake his wife had made, and gave me some wise advice on my community initiative I ran by him.

I don't think I asked particularly coherent questions, but I do recall him telling me that he rarely said yes to meeting up with relative strangers, and that I was riding on the coattails of someone very dear to him, who helped him in his first job in the publishing industry.

When I asked him what her name was, it had absolutely no relation to mine, but I didn't care. I was here, having tea with Seth!

I have very fond memories of that meetup, and all because I had an intention, a strong desire, and a will to make it happen, backed up by consistent and focused action. In other words I made the 'schlep' (love that word).

So, gorgeous, what is it that you want? Get really clear on that and then go ahead and ask for it. Envision the outcome you want, and smile.

PS I asked him on my podcast a year later and he actually said yes to that too.

Whether or not you think I sound like a stalker, the moral of this chapter is that when your intentions align with your action and determination, almost *anything* you want to happen can actually happen. The trick is to be creative in finding the solution, be clear in your request of the person, organisation, or universe, and be unwavering in your pursuit.

Most people give up at the first rejection, decline, or hurdle. Be in the 1% who never gives up, especially not on yourself. You're worth it.

ENERGY VAMPIRE REMEDIES

You know what I find scariest in this world? Humans disguised as humans when, in fact, they are energy vampires. Not the ones you see in *Twilight*. I'm talking about the vampires in your everyday life.

Oh yes, didn't you know? They're all around you. Sucking away at the life and soul of you, sometimes without you even realising.

Unlike 'real' vampires, they don't just bite your neck and drain you of all your blood in one foul swoop. Oh no, they drain you of your life force slowly, painfully, one drop at a time, until you realise you are just a former version of your effervescent self, and completely spent.

HOW DO YOU SPOT AN ENERGY VAMPIRE?

They typically come in the form of friends, family, and well-intentioned colleagues or peers whose energy is so heavy you feel the weight of them on your shoulders the minute they walk in the room or enter your personal space, and who simply suck the life out of you.

They typically start speaking something like this:

> Hi girl, oh you wouldn't believe the day I had. First of all, my washing machine stopped working on me, right when I needed fresh underwear most. Then I missed my bus to work, so I was super late. Which then meant my boss was pissed with me…again. And she's given me a warning. I mean, the cheek of it. I'm rarely late, well yeah, only a few times a week. And here she is telling me that I don't honour time commitments, I don't respect the team or her, and I don't respect working hours. I mean really, b*tch. I hate her. I hate my job. I hate my life right now. You know?

Note that they haven't checked in on how you are because they're so self-absorbed in their own shitty problems, which they've caused themselves. And to make matters worse, in just a few short seconds they've overwhelmed you with their drama, which you feel compelled to help them overcome, or at least offer support and compassion.

I'm telling you not to. I know, it sounds harsh. But trust me, if you start, they'll never stop sucking on your support and compassion.

Another way you can identify energy vampires is by how they can extinguish a perfectly wonderful moment, in an instant.

Here's an example. You've just finished telling your friend that you're feeling really grateful about life right now, because you've taken on some new clients, and your revenue is picking up, and you're feeling like you're finally gathering momentum. Midway through, they cut you off without any hesitancy, with an invisible filter that seems to swallow up your good news:

'Well isn't that great for you. I mean, it's soooo good that your life is going so well [said in a sarcastic tone], while mine is positively shit. I really don't appreciate you gloating over why your life is so freaking awesome right now, when mine is such a mess. Couldn't you spend some time listening to me for once, and giving me some advice on how to fix my problems?'

If you're saying to yourself, 'Oh my god, I have those types of vampires/friends in my life!' then girl, we need to make a plan to get rid of the energy vampires before you give them even more energy and they eat you alive.

The great news is that it doesn't require you buying any garlic, wooden stakes, or metal crosses to get rid of them (although you could try that just for shits and giggles). But make no mistake—we do need to get them out of your life, because there's no use trying to 'fix' these vampires. They simply don't want to be fixed.

Energy vampires revel in self-pity, they wallow in despair, they chew up hope and spit it out. They won't ever take responsibility or do any work on their own personal growth. They will just continue to feed on happy, healthy, positive, forward-thinking, compassionate, kind humans, for as long as they shall live—and vampires live a long and miserable life!

ENERGY VAMPIRES WANT TO SUCK YOU DRY

I don't have any time for vampires. I can typically spot them a mile away, because I've been bitten badly before. When somebody is affecting your happiness, it is time to let them go. It's as simple as saying goodbye, but I know there's a little voice inside your head saying, 'Natalie, that is not simple'.

But it is. And here's why. Energy vampires are toxic.

According to women's health expert Dr Christine Northrup, they're sources of chronic stress, which means you're putting yourself at a higher risk of chronic problems ranging from autoimmune diseases to heart disease, obesity, and depression. This is especially so if the energy vampire is someone you can't avoid—like a spouse, a parent, a sibling, or your best friend's friend—because that individual is constantly draining your energy.

So now we've established that your happiness, energy, and well-being depend on ridding your life of energy vampires, I need to hammer home one more thing. This isn't you being selfish or cruel; you're actually practicing life-saving techniques here that will save you from getting overwhelmed, anxious, and sick, because energy vampires are a genuine health risk, and the longer you leave them in your life, the more chance you give them to make you physically and mentally sick.

Try these methods to banish energy vampires for good.

Step One: Redirect your energy toward people in your life who share your values.

Start hanging out with the friends and other people who bring you happiness, who bring you joy, who stretch you, who push you in the best possible ways, and who bring out the best in you. When you start redirecting your energy toward them, the universe will begin redirecting their energy to you and you start to meet more of those people in your life and surround yourself with the people who are awesome.

Step Two: Know that toxic people won't change. It's their problem, not yours.

Knowing in your heart of hearts that they're not going to change until they actually want to change, that enables you to spend less time and energy trying to convince them that life is great when instead they're just pulling you down.

Step Three: Block your energy vampires on social media, and even on your phone.

It's an easy step not to see their posts about why they're miserable, or read about something they just want to have a rant about. That way, it's far less likely that their destructive energy is going to impact you. You just don't need their negativity.

Instead come back to step one, which is replacing them with people who do have the right energy and who share your values. Start following futurists, writers, inspirational people who totally make your day. It'll change your whole world if, instead of vampires, your news feed is full of positive world-changing people who are making a difference.

Step Four: Stick to your boundaries and values.

You can distance these vampires at any time, yes even family members. You can say to yourself 'Enough'. You can say, 'Enough. I'm not going to the movies with them this weekend because they're going to talk the whole way through and bitch about the actors and why it's shitty. Instead, I'm gonna go along with this really cool person who just happens to love this director and we're gonna have a great time at the movie'.

You can also be really, really clear in your determination that you just don't have time for people who are ranting, who are racist, who are sexist, or any other 'ist' that isn't within your value set.

It is your choice about who you spend your time with. Time is precious. You have the same amount of it as they do, but if they're wasting their life complaining about stuff that is not within their control (or is within their control but they refuse to fix it) and it's affecting your happiness, then please set those boundaries. Limit the amount of time you spend with them and start hanging out with frankly cooler people.

BE YOUR OWN HEROINE

'I just want to help everyone', a gorgeous member of the $10K Club said on one of our group coaching calls. She went on to explain that once her business grew, she couldn't wait to hire a woman she'd worked with on her team, and who was just amazing.

I asked her why she couldn't hire her now, or someone else, to help her out in her business so she could focus on what she did best. The response was one I hear all too often, and have even uttered myself in a past life: 'I need to make sure she's taken care of, is paid well, and can provide for her family. I will be fully responsible for her, as I don't want her to suffer or miss out if I can't afford to pay her'.

I stopped her right there, and because she's open to learning like crazy, she listened and understood when I explained, 'You are not responsible for anyone else's life but yours. You do not need to rescue her; you need to empower her to do a great job. But let's get this straight—

you only need to focus on being your own heroine, not anyone else's'.

She got it, and it was a powerful moment for everyone on the call, because as women, we are always thinking about others, putting them before us, and taking on their problems as if they are our own.

No more. No freaking more!

You don't serve anybody by doing that. Instead you weaken your own defences, burn through your energy, create less space for your growth, and become a victim to others' issues.

Despite preaching this great advice, I had repeatedly fallen victim to playing the heroine, rescuing my clients and customers far too many times over the years. I really had to learn this for myself the hard way, because I cared *so much* about the transformations of my clients and students that I was doing everything I could to help them out: following up with personalised emails to see how they were getting on in launching their own courses, reaching out across multiple social channels to check in on them when they'd gone missing during a live course, making myself extremely available anytime for feedback or advice.

I won't lie; this is a part of my style that I think sets me apart in a sea of sameness as a business, life, and mindset coach. However, it comes at a price, which at the time I was not charging or valuing enough.

Instead, I needed to recognise, as you may need to, that I am not responsible for someone else's results, behaviour, or outcomes. No matter how much you care or 'try', you are not them. They need to go on their own journey, at their own pace, and discover for themselves what they need to learn, in order to progress and evolve.

There is still a lot you can do for others:

- You can hold space for them, create a safe container that allows them to grow and evolve, stretch and learn.

- You can guide them lovingly with your leadership and wisdom.

- You can provide them with encouragement, motivation, and support.

- You can believe in them fully and shine a light on their infinite potential.

But you cannot *be* them or get them to where they need to be. That's entirely up to them.

If you need a strong visual to anchor to this, to remind yourself to be your own heroine and not anyone else's, then think of Princess Diana, also known as Wonder Woman.

Upon learning of a war, she ventures into the world of men to stop Ares, the god of war, from destroying mankind. That was her first mistake—attempting to stop men, rather than focusing on hanging with her all-female Amazonian race of kickass women, but I digress.

The heartache, tragedy, and loss she experiences in trying to rescue men from themselves, including her hunky pilot Steve, is just too much. Sure, she eventually saves the world, but at what cost?

This might seem a tad dramatic, or perhaps you're not into superheroes, yet when you apply this to your everyday life, you can hopefully start to see how often you rush in to save, defend, and rescue your friends, family, peers, team, clients, and even strangers, without thinking about the consequences.

Your brilliance, your precious time, your amazing gifts, your boundless energy are best used to superpower yourself first, and then ripple out to help others who are ready to take action and be responsible for their own lives.

Now go have a heroine break, a siesta, a bubble bath, or a massage. You deserve it.

LEARN TO LOVE FAILURE

It was late October 2018, and not long after a pretty successful launch of my second bestselling book, *The Freedom Plan: Redesign Your Business to Work Less, Earn More and Be Free.*

I decided to relaunch my most successful course ever of the same name that, to date, netted me over US$500,000 in sales. Except this time, I totally redesigned and upgraded it to better align with my new book and to be more focused on how to work less through systems, outsourcing, and clever sales funnels.

It catered to an experienced business owner wanting more freedom—the folks I wanted to work with because I could see them experiencing burnout and overwhelm and I truly wanted to help them. Yet in doing so, I overlooked the majority of my community I'd lovingly built up over the years, who in reality were still wanting to build their online business, learn how to earn more money, and gain financial freedom.

The launch result? *I failed in an epic way.*

I was expecting over 50 sales and I made eight. That hurt, a lot, especially since the previous course was double the price and I sold to over 200 wonderful people.

I cried in the final days of launch and then sat there in disbelief as literally nothing happened—at least that's what it felt like. It caused me to doubt everything I thought I knew and was really good at, built up over nine years of business.

I was in shock. I was numb. I felt like a fraud. The facts didn't help either. I'd spent too much money, hired too many people, and ended up handing over most of the things I'm great at, and got stuck with managing people, logistics, and operations.

Along with that, I had not listened to my intuition and how I felt energetically, and forged on regardless, because I wanted to stay true to my word and launch the course that I promised I would—damn upholder in me!

Even worse, I didn't follow my tried and true method that I loved: preselling the course before creating the damn thing, to validate that it's what people actually want and need! I instead followed a proven launch method that does work, but I didn't line up energetically with. It felt too forced, too polished. Not my style at all.

When I did my launch analysis, which I do faithfully every time, it wasn't as bad as I thought; the conversions for the traffic and leads I had were on industry average, but I just hadn't gotten enough of them. Truthfully, my own lack of belief had sabotaged my results too. I'm a huge believer that where focus goes, energy flows, and I was focused on all the fear and doubt. The damage was done. My confidence was knocked and I wasn't bouncing back like I normally do.

Can you relate?

I was desperately trying to find the lesson in the failure. A smart entrepreneur will always do that, but I was taking it way too personally. After almost a decade it felt like I'd made a rookie error and it had cost me more than just money and a bruised ego.

THE TRUTH WAS, I WANTED TO QUIT MY BUSINESS.

Deep down I was quite tired of my business. I'm sure I'm not alone when I admit this.

For most of my business journey I've loved every aspect of my business, but there's only so long one can continue to talk about the same thing all the time before getting a little bored, stifled, or jaded.

Despite continuing to learn, I had gotten comfortable in my knowledge and expertise and was looking for a challenge. Most of the time I had managed to find that within and apply it to my journey and clients. But with all the massive life changes I'd experienced, and the time off I had taken from my business in 2017, I had never really found my flow again. I felt like I was holding onto something that I wasn't passionate about anymore.

Here's the big thing I learned. If you fail, it means nothing. It simply means you failed this one time with this one experience.

THERE IS NO SUCH THING AS FAILURE, ONLY FAILURE TO LEARN THE LESSON.

I took the time to actually understand what the heck went wrong, and why I reacted so poorly to it, and how I could learn from it. I ran the gamut, reviewing my history of successful six-figure launches, and released that version of myself, to make way for the new version of Natalie who was relearning and learning new things.

I got brave and talked about it openly on my blog and on my podcast, to my clients, friends, and peers, so that I could focus on the freedom of being my true self. And it was so cathartic to be that authentic, vulnerable, and transparent with my community. People love a peek behind the scenes, especially when it's not all sunshine and roses.

I'm someone who prides herself on launching, and far from painting me as a loser who screwed up a launch, I found that people were so appreciative that I showed a human face and disclosed the reality of running your own business. I was able to demonstrate that sometimes— perhaps more often than we realise—we make mistakes, and they're painful.

So much of the time we are too focused on putting on our 'best face' and only sharing the good happening in our lives, like we're on a stage putting on a performance. But if we invested our time into taking the learning from the experience, we are actually able to move through it and get on with life a lot more quickly, and be stronger for it.

If we surrender to the process and work through it, and surround ourselves with people who support us on this journey, it can be the most liberating time ever.

A huge positive that came out of this experience was that nine months later I created the Launch Your Damn Course Accelerator in the complete opposite fashion. I followed my own launch style, which was simple and effective. I presold to ten people before I even created it, and then created the course as I went.

I filmed it all myself in our 'shed' that I'd turned into a studio. I taught on what I knew to be true and drew on all my knowledge of launches. I didn't refer to anyone else's launch stuff; I went offline to develop my own signature style and content based on my years of experience and results.

I followed my own approach. Created the sales page and the design myself. Used Canva to design in-depth and beautiful workbooks. And basically built the whole thing myself and *loved* it.

My energy was high, my passion for it was undeniable, and it's gone on to become one of my most popular and effective courses.

Now my team works with me to manage all the moving parts so I can turn up and deliver the best live coaching and advice. Together, we make every launch and make it bigger and better. I wouldn't have built it that way or created something I loved had I not experienced the pain of doing my other launch using someone else's method, and experiencing the pain of a launch that flopped.

Trust your gut. Do it your way. Be true to you.

IGNORE THE NAYSAYERS

Don't you just love those people who tell you what you can't do?

That your business idea sucks

That you're not capable of doing a 5km run

That you will never write a book

That your idea to quit your job and travel the world is a terrible one

No. Me neither.

I'm talking about the naysayers of the world, which sounds like a medieval word that we should ignore, and the kind of people we need to ignore too.

The Merriam-Webster definition and example of a naysayer is:

> *one who denies, refuses, opposes, or is skeptical or cynical about something*

> There are always naysayers who say it can't
> be done.

You might recognise this definition in a loved one, a family member, a friend or two, in your community, your work, your business—they're all around us. They're waiting to tell us what we really don't want or need to hear.

I had a lovely member of my $10K Club say, 'Nat, how do you ignore the naysayers?'.

'You ignore them'.

If I wanted to write the world's shortest chapter, that would be my straight-up, honest answer. Obviously, I didn't stop there. I asked her about the naysayer who was causing her grief.

Turns out it was her husband on this occasion. He didn't believe her new business was a good thing to launch into, despite the fact that she was already very successful in business—with him! She gave an example of a conversation they had where he'd clearly hurt her by not having faith in her abilities. I asked her how she responded.

'Oh I told him to quit being such a wet rag, and that this was important to me, and that I needed his full support. I went on to say that I have all the doubts and fears he's mentioned, and I don't need someone else reinforcing them. I need him to tell me all the reasons why I *can* totally do this, and share examples of where I've already done this before. I explained the research and due diligence

I'd done to get to this point, as well as my vision for how it would help us out financially, and then I reminded him one more time to pull up his socks and show me some love and support.'

'Perfect', I replied with a big grin on my face. 'You did everything I was going to advise you to do as your coach:

- You called him out.

- Then you explained why this was important to you.

- You gave valid reasons that benefited not only you, but him.

- Then you asked him for what you need.

'The only step I'd add is be specific on how you'd like him to help you, as in, 'When I start talking about x, lovingly pull me aside and say that's not true; you've got this'.

She laughed too, as she realised she'd done her part. Now it was up to him to join her on her new adventure, which he has.

THE REAL REASON PEOPLE ARE NAYSAYERS

People who try to squish your hopes and dreams before you've even had a chance to pursue them are not outright total pricks. What they are, though, is projecting their own hopes and fears *on to you*.

They see you being brave, and wanting to start something new or take a leap of faith, and they want to protect you from getting hurt. So they decide hurting you early on is a great idea, because that will deter you from doing what you want.

Not ideal, I know, but it seems logical to them. Nine times out of ten, a naysayer is wanting to protect you.

My advice is to go easy, and break it to them gently that you're going to do this regardless. If they don't want to support you, that's their choice, but they can get out of your damn way so you can go galloping off on your trusty steed, to the adventure that awaits you! (I got all caught up in medieval fairy tale there, but you get my gist.)

The other one time out of ten, they are just being a total meanie. They might be jealous, because you're doing something they told themselves long ago they weren't capable of. They might be the most cynical person in the world, because nothing has ever gone their way (they made this their reality, by the way), so why should you have all the fun?

The next time a well-intentioned but pain-in-the-ass friend or family member tells you all about the reason the thing you want to do is not going to work out, ask whether they have experience in this area. For example:

You: 'I'm going to start a new fitness business and help women who want to train for triathlons get into peak shape'.

Them: 'Ohhhh, I don't know about that, love. I mean, you've only just got your personal trainer qualification. You need some practical experience first. You can't just start a business. Plus personal trainers don't typically earn that much. Why don't you get a job in law like you wanted to as a kid? That pays well and it's a reputable profession.'

Your two options to respond:

OPTION 1. Stomp your feet, get angry, and tell them to piss off; they don't know what they're talking about. *(This probably won't help anybody, and it's likely a triggered response to a lifetime of being told what you can and can't do.)*

OPTION 2: Genuinely thank them for their opinion and their concern. Then get curious about why they're saying this.

'Thanks, Dad. The thing is, you know I've been passionate about health and fitness since I was a kid. And you know I've been competing in triathlons for years and how much joy, confidence, and awesome friends it's brought me. You also know I've been wanting to start a business where I'm fully independent to do the work I love, earn what I'm worth, and work with people I really want to help.

'I've done my research and there's a local gym happy to have me base myself out of their offices. The monthly rental cost is tiny compared to me finding my own place. Plus I will be in the perfect place to get in front of the clients I want to help most.

'There's only upside here. So you have no need to be concerned. You raised me to be a great kid, and now I'm going to continue being a great adult. Watch and see. I got this. More importantly, I'll do even better in business with your full support and blessing behind me'.

If you got this far, well done, they're listening. If they then open their mouths to object again simply say:

'Look, I'm passionate about this and excited. I thought you'd be happy for me. However, if you'd rather sit there and tell me otherwise, then know this: I won't be needing any further "advice" from you. I'll turn to people who have actual experience in starting and growing a business'.

Then turn and walk away.

Granted you won't get this right every time. It won't go as you planned in the dialogue you're having in your head right now. But know that by keeping calm, being compassionate yet firm with them, and showing them you're going ahead anyway, they will eventually come around.

And if they're too stubborn, irrational, or cyclical to support you, then create real distance between you until they get the message.

Life's too short to hang out with naysayers. Go do your thang!

SURF THE WAVES OF LIFE

It's a gorgeous hot, sunny day and I'm sitting on a surfboard floating over a reef, which is currently well submerged by beautiful clear green waters at high tide, and looking back at the beach of Baleal, Portugal.

Out here, in nature, I feel free. My mind is clear, focused, and still. I'm in my happy place. This is my sixth surf lesson, and today our teacher is Craig, the friendly Australian from Surfers Paradise. Earlier, in the surf shop, while we put on our wetsuits and got assigned our giant foam beginner boards, he told us we were in for a treat.

'Why's that?' I ask.

'Cos today we're going to legit.'

'Legit? Aren't all the surf spots around here legit?'

'Nah mate, leeeegitttttt'. And he proceeded to tell us that 'Lagide' is a specific surf spot where the waves consistently roll over the top of a reef, and that if you time it right and the conditions are perfect, you'll experience an epic surf session.

Up to this point, Josh and I, new to surfing, had barely managed to stand up for more than a few seconds in our lessons. In fact, surfing was way harder than I imagined, even with my sporting background. I had an entitled Princess attitude on the first day, that I should be good at surfing—and promptly had that belief smacked out of me on my first attempt at paddling out!

Up until now, we had mainly experienced inhaling a lot of cold water, being dumped by waves, smacked on the head by our surfboard, and more failed attempts to ride a wave than I imagined possible in a two-hour lesson.

Yet today the sun was shining, and Craig's boundless enthusiasm and toothy grin had me thinking that this might indeed be an epic surf day.

Once in the cool water, we paddled out back, past the reef, and sat on our boards, feeling like characters in the movie *Point Break* watching Craig explain where we were going to enter the wave and how we were going to paddle when the sets rolled in.

He made it all sound so easy, and then to prove a point, as a wave started building behind us, he lay down and effortlessly paddled in across to the centre and then, in one smooth and elegant move, he was up on his board and racing down the front of the wave, like he was dancing on water.

Josh and I and the other tourist joining us in the lesson all looked on in admiration of this demonstration, then looked at each other and shrugged in agreement that we had no idea how to make it look that easy, but what the heck. We looked back at Craig, who was now at the shore, signalling with excited hand movements that it was our turn next.

I took a deep breath, lay down, and started to remember all I'd learned in the previous lessons, kicking and paddling, turning my head back over my shoulder to watch the incoming wave and line up with it, to time it just right (a rare thing for me).

And then I saw it, the perfect wave. Not too big, not too small, and coming right my way. I took another deep breath and heard in my mind Nelson, the founder of this surf school, yelling at me in his strong Portuguese accent: 'Naaaat, paddle, paddle, paddle!'

So I did, with all my might, and that beautiful wave, she picked me up just as I jumped up onto my board in one movement. I let her gently guide me while I soared on top, the entire way to the shore.

It felt like it lasted a lifetime. In reality it was probably only seven seconds, but it was the longest time I had ever managed to stay up on a board. She was the first wave I rode from beginning to end and she even let me gracefully dismount by myself, unlike previous waves that threw me into the surf.

I was on cloud nine. I yelled out in sheer freaking joy. I was grinning from ear to ear, and so was Craig. Josh cheered me from back where I had started this epic journey, and in that moment I realised why people fell in love with surfing.

In that moment, nothing else mattered. I wasn't caught up with thoughts in my head, or feeling anxious, or worried, or judging myself. I was nowhere else but right there, in nature, dancing on the ocean's wave and being truly present.

For the next two hours, I managed to catch nothing short of eight waves (a new record) from start to finish, until I was so elated and exhausted that I couldn't actually paddle out anymore. I finally got what it meant to be in flow when it came to surfing, and the high lasted for hours.

The next day, it was off to another surf beach with Pedro. I felt like a legitimate surfer, brimming with confidence, and I was *so* ready to take on this lesson and continue to bond with the ocean and my board. In fact I was already channeling my inner Paige Alms, a Maui big-wave surfer who's self-taught and she's one helluva role model.

Conditions were different today. This beach was rocky, it was less sunny, the wind had picked up, and the waves looked, well, gnarly. Yet I had this inner confidence and that I was now a bona fide surfer.

We did our beach warm up and Pedro gently guided us through how this surf spot worked, drawing patterns and building up model waves in the sand to show us what we were going to be doing. I was so keen to get in the water that I was the first out with Pedro, and he sensed it, so when the first wave came along, he said calmly, 'Go get it, Nat'.

Heck yeah, I was going to go get it. Except the wave had other plans for me.

I paddled like crazy and was up in a flash, and the next second I was face down in the water, tumbling in the crashing wave that swallowed me up, tossed me around, and spat me out five seconds later.

Gasping for air, I came up to the surface, looking for my board, coughing and spluttering and completely confused. I'd almost run out of breath and had hit the bottom badly. I was visibly shaken, but more than anything my ego was bruised.

That wave, she had taught me a lesson, and made it clear I needed to know who was boss. She said to me: Don't ever disrespect the power of the ocean, don't ever think you're too big for your wetsuit boots, and don't you dare think that just because you had an awesome day yesterday that today is going to be more sunshine and roses.

I proceeded to miss every single wave that rolled in, or get smashed by them. It was soul destroying and I was exhausted. I gave up after 45 minutes and went and sat on the beach. After coughing up some more salt water, I checked in on my bruised ego and realised this was very much a Suck It Up, Princess moment.

I took time to reflect more on the other lessons she'd taught me that day. That when she knocked me off and tossed me around in the ocean, that was my moment to rise up, to be resilient, and to fight for what I wanted—air, and then another opportunity to try again.

Not from a place of 'This should be easy and I should be able to surf, dammit', but from a place of 'Okay, thanks for the lesson. I know what I need to do: stay calm, breathe, be present, be ready, and I'm ready to seize the next opportunity you give me'.

She had taught me to find inner strength, and to keep going back for more punishment, as that simply made me stronger. Yep, I thought to myself, that was the lesson I needed to learn today. Thank you, lady ocean, for teaching it to me so well.

I realised another reason why people love surfing so much. It teaches you to be present, to go with the flow, to surrender to the moment, and learn from it. You also develop a tremendous amount of emotional resilience; you simply can't be all 'up in your head' when you're out on the ocean. You can't make it personal. If you get taken out by a wave or fall off your board, you have to say, 'Suck It Up, Princess' and get right back on.

American professor and mindfulness master Jon Kabat-Zinn once said you cannot stop the waves, but you can learn to surf. And that's precisely what I was here to do, and always will be. We all get thrown in the deep end at some point in our life. The question is, how long are you going to take to quit flailing about and start swimming in the direction you want to go in your life?

QUIT JUDGING EVERYTHING

After a meditation one morning, I wrote this in my journal:

> The higher version of myself shows courage, leads by example, is fun, fearless, and compassionate. She's focused on her dreams and makes them happen, through her goals and LifePilot methodology.

I went on to note that I was in fact nitpicking in my mind about Josh's lack of morning routine, exercise, or care about—well, most things that were important to me around the house. I noticed that some of it was true, but most of it was me judging by my own high standards. I needed to change, if I was to break this cycle and focus instead on having a wonderful, inspired life.

Less than nine days later I found myself at a personal development event designed to bring about positive, permanent shifts in the quality of your life.

You see, I had chosen to invest over $30,000 in myself in one year, to grow both personally and professionally and immerse myself in training, strategies, and experiences to see what magic could happen. This was the first event on the calendar, and a great way to kick off January.

The second day in, I found myself being called up to the stage, supposedly to offer advice on another forum participant's challenge, and suddenly realising I was now 'one of those people': exposed, in the spotlight, about to have an intervention thanks to the coach to strip me of my ego, and get me back to my pure, essential me—that's how it felt after seeing numerous others go through the same thing.

It may sound harsh, but it's a bit like a Suck It Up, Princess moment, except you get coaching and a slap of reality at the same time!

Ten minutes later, after bringing my deepest insecurities (aka ego) to the open, being radically honest about myself and my behaviour in relationships, crying, releasing, and reframing...

There I was. A new woman. With an audience of 84 others all cheering me on, being touched and inspired too and coming up to me during the break to thank me.

Apparently they were all judgemental human beings too, and by me admitting this on stage, for all to see, they were able to realise they'd been doing the same with people they loved and cared for.

I phoned Josh immediately after my 'breakthrough', while it was fresh and raw. I told him:

1. I've been pretending to motivate and encourage you to be your best self.

2. In fact, I've been demeaning you or making you feel small, so that I could feel superior about myself.

3. The impact of that inauthentic way of being and acting is that I hurt and criticise you, and push you away, and that I feel like a horrible person.

4. The whole time I've been being and acting this way, what's been missing is any sense of true connection, love, and understanding.

5. Standing here, the possibility I am inventing for myself and my life (and ours) is one of true love, acceptance, and compassion.

I had tears rolling down my face and stayed quiet to hear Josh's response. Being the amazing human he is, he immediately said, 'Oh babe, I love you, and I just want to give you a big virtual hug. Thank you for sharing. I feel you're being a bit harsh on yourself, but I do acknowledge that yes there's truth in what you're saying'.

When I got home a few days later, it was like seeing him and our relationship (and life, basically) through a very different lens. It was lighter, more beautiful, more real.

All I saw was what I loved about Josh. I still do. And sure those moments of judgement will creep up, but I can catch them, see them for what they are, and replace those thoughts in an instant, to focus on reality.

Whenever I feel judgemental, I hold a mirror up to my face (sometimes physically, most of the time metaphorically) and seek to learn 'What is this saying about me? What do I need to look at within myself that's not in alignment?'

That's when I find the real truth, and can be honest with myself, and come from a place of understanding and compassion. Works *every* time.

Try it out yourself. Mirror, mirror on the wall, what is this really saying about me?

CALLING YOURSELF
IN AND OUT

I'm a big fan of calling myself out on my own bullshit, like:

> 'Come on, Natalie, quit faffing around and get this bloody book written, will ya? You've had plenty of time to dedicate to writing, and you're choosing to get distracted and do other things. Get cracking!'

Yep, I literally have those conversations with myself when I'm fed up with my inability to finish something that is actually important. If I really want to call myself out, I will post publicly to state what I'm going to commit to, so that I now have a really good reason to make it happen.

As an Upholder (according to the Four Tendencies Quiz from Gretchen Rubin, which reveals how you respond to expectations), I have great internal and external accountability. So I make doubly sure by doing that public posting that I don't disappoint myself or my peers.

I also appreciate when friends and other people I trust and admire call me out if I don't see the errors in my ways, even though I don't love the feeling when it happens. I mean, who does love being told they're acting like a first-class ignoramus?!

I genuinely wish more people would have the self-awareness and emotional capacity to call themselves out more often. And I wish more people would stand up for what they believe and call out bad behaviour, like this:

> 'Hey, I know this isn't what you want to hear, but you have to stop cheating on your partner, grow up, own up to this, and act like the adult you are. You're hurting them, and your kids, and yourself in your actions'.

> Or 'I really don't like it when you slag off marketers as if they're all evil people. Marketing is an art, and when done well, it can change people's lives by helping them make informed choices with what they read, buy, or invest in'.

If someone is making you feel uncomfortable because what they do or say or how they act is fundamentally out of alignment with the values you hold true to in this world, or they're just outright rude, hurtful, or even harmful to yourself or others, call them out on it. If they can't handle the truth, aren't willing to discuss it, or refuse to see reason (whether in the moment or after some time out), then they're probably not a great person to have in your life.

An alternative is calling in, which aims to get you, or the person you feel needs it, to change their problematic behaviour.

The primary difference between calling in and calling out—in the context of you doing this to yourself and others—is that calling in is done with a little more compassion and patience. It really hurts and it can shock you to your core, depending on how it's done, like when a former client called me in for not using my platform and influence to better support the #blacklivesmatter movement.

What ensued was all the normal behaviours and feeling that my white fragility allowed me to have, like defending myself as a good person, and denying that I was part of the oppressive and systemic racist system that existed.

It was deep, heavy, emotionally exhausting as I began to dismantle my sense of white supremacy. It took a few weeks of some real soul-searching, conversations with friends, and a whole lotta education (ongoing for life), before I was able to step out of victim mode and into my power to do something useful, valuable, and helpful.

This meant changing policies and guidelines in my business and community around equity, inclusion, and diversity. It meant levelling up my entire perspective on how I wanted to act and show up, and who I wanted to support, promote, interview, and shine a light on.

In my personal life it meant recognizing everything I had grown up with for what it really was, and questioning my worldview and perspectives, my circle of friends and peers, and whether all of this was in alignment with who I wanted to be, and how I wanted to show up in the world.

It's turned out to be a gift. The transformation I've been on, the learning I've undertaken, the actions and allyship I continue to undertake have been life-changing for me and others in my community. Sure I've likely lost or will lose friends, clients, and community members, but that seems like a small price to pay to be part of an equitable and just world.

The thing is, there ain't no growth if you can't see how your actions, behaviours, or beliefs are hurting you and others. There's a reason they're called blind spots.

THE ART OF DELIVERING THE TRUTH TO YOURSELF AND OTHERS

I've learned over the years when to be a little gentler with myself, and to reason with where I'm at:

> 'Hey Nat, I know this has been a big week, and I know you've given your all. You deserve a rest and to celebrate, but if you can just finish this final step,

you know you're going to feel so much better about this whole project. Let's do this'.

Or doing this publicly, I'll post an honest assessment of where I'm at and what I'm not doing, and ask people for their advice or support.

You're still calling yourself out, but you're doing it in a way that asks for help. I used to struggle with this, but people genuinely want to help and suggest solutions.

As a coach, educator, and leader, I have no problem calling in my clients and community, especially when someone questions my integrity, which is my number one highest value in life. I love the results you can achieve when you do this well, and if the person is open to a discussion or willing to listen to your point of view, and assess their own.

I've turned around vehement email subscribers in my community from people who think it's a good idea to send me an abusive email into diehard fans.

I've helped people who comment on my blog to see how they could have better handled an outburst of anger, jealousy, or malice, and be a better contributor.

I've helped people who had a mini breakdown at a retreat to come out feeling nourished, supported, and empowered.

I relish the opportunity to show them some compassion, and get to the heart of what's really bothering them, rather than taking it personally (which believe me is a work in progress).

Here's an email thread example of me doing this with love:

> Hi Natalie.
>
> I love what you are doing and I love XXX.
>
> BUT using XXX as an example of someone making $1500 in a week without saying how many people are already in her community and the paid group is not really a fair lead-in for selling your training.
>
> I expect better from you ;-)
>
> Bet your training is amazing!!!!
>
> Have a blast
>
>> Hey
>>
>> Surprised to get this email.
>>
>> XXX gladly gave that testimonial as she'd been aiming to launch her course for 2.5 years and finally did it in 8 weeks.
>>
>> She worked really hard on doing everything in my accelerator, and turning up to the calls and did amazingly.

Second, despite having a huge group, she realised she had not put much time and effort at all into her email list or marketing, so it was quite a challenge for her.

You may recall in the group she launched to crickets, and to her credit, completely rethought her strategy and offering a week later to get to this result.

So I expect better from you than to assume you know the real deal.

Natalie

Hi Natalie,

Sorry if it came across that way. It was an initial reaction first thing in the morning and I should learn not to share my thoughts at that point.

I don't want to take anything away from how hard both of you work, on everything you do. And I believe what you both put out in the world is awesome.

Thanks for calling me out on how I responded.

I think I should check myself to figure out what's really bothering me—about me!

Thank you

And that's that. Both of us walk away respecting each other with our integrity intact.

So, my fair lady, it's time to ask yourself:

- Where do you need to step up and be more honest with yourself and with others?

- Where do you need to show up fearlessly and say what needs to be said?

- Who do you need to call in or out, and how can you do this lovingly and respectfully?

BURNOUT IS NOT A BADGE OF HONOUR

Burnout is the secret enemy that emerges when our need and desire to 'do it all' or 'be perfect' is taking center stage. Burnout is something that everyone needs to start paying more attention to, otherwise it will take you, and all your hard work, down in a flame of—well, no glory.

If you feel like:

- You are doing too much in life and don't know how to stop.

- You have not been able to pause and reflect and enjoy the present moment.

- You are constantly thinking, processing, and on the go and can't switch off your busy mind.

- Everything is compounding and piling up on you.

- You believe you could be superwoman in disguise as you're on fire in everything you do.

Then it's quite likely you're heading toward burnout, and fast. By the way, that last symptom is the most dangerous because it's usually a sure sign that you're about to collapse. I want to stop you before you get there, because your health, your energy, and your life is way more important than being overworked and trying to take on too much.

MY BRUSH WITH BURNOUT

I first experienced what burnout felt like on my 2013 *Suitcase Entrepreneur* book tour through the US and Canada.

I had been obsessing about this book and its launch for months. With all the endless marketing, PR, interviews, and community building around it, I was riding high on all the goodwill and attention because, deep down, I really wanted this book to impact a *lot* of people.

It all worked out and it became a No #1 Bestseller on Amazon in three categories and to date has sold over 30,000 copies and thousands of audiobooks. But it also worked to the detriment of my health in the form of mild burnout.

Burnout is not fun at all. You are so lethargic you can't do anything. Everything takes effort. It hurts to think. You overreact to the smallest things. You're emotional. You really are good for nothing. And that's just mild burnout!

What's worse, it took two dear friends, Karley and Elise, to recognise it in me, and force me to stop working night and day. They noticed I was running full tilt and operating over 120% and they were naturally a little worried about me.

'Hey Nat,' they asked, 'have you had a decent night's sleep lately?' You're looking tired and you're acting a bit highly strung. You're just like go, go, go girl and it doesn't seem like you're switching off. And that's not sustainable'.

My response: 'Oh no, I've got this. I'm totally fine'.

They thankfully ignored me and made me leave my devices behind, disconnect, and join them in the park to eat fish and chips and simply sit and watch the sunset.

We sat there for about two hours, and I could feel the release of the stress melting away. I could sense my brain start to slow down and I began just to be present in that moment, enjoying the peace, quiet, and tranquility, the birds and that stunning sunset.

In that moment I grasped how exhausted I was and how I had not stopped. I realised that I was working 18-hour days, constantly working on anything and everything to help this book be a success. Talking about burnout that night and understanding what I was heading for was my saving grace and sparked my road to recovery.

If you can see yourself in this story, and it sounds like where you're at right now, please note that this may be a sign that you are very, very close to burning out or potentially already there and you haven't given yourself space to heal.

So I want to get really honest with you about burnout, which is way more common than it should be, and more importantly, how to spot it before it bites you in the ass!

WHAT LEADS TO BURNOUT?

A *Harvard Business Review* article, 'What Makes Entre-preneurs Burn Out', researched over 300 entrepreneurs and found the following:

The obsessively passionate entrepreneurs reported feeling that work was more emotionally draining and that working all day required a great deal of effort. They indicated feeling frustrated by their work and even that it was breaking them down. For some, their burnout caused a constant state of anxiety and stress. Those with an obsessive passion and a fixed mindset were even more prone to burnout.

If you found yourself nodding your head at any of those findings, listen up.

When it comes to being a woman entrepreneur, career professional, or full-time working mum, one of the hardest things to do is to slow the heck down. We often don't realise how much we pack into our daily lives. Not only our own passions, projects, and ideas, but taking on everyone else' responsibilities because, let's face it, deep down we are superwomen and can do so much in a given day.

But the more focused you are, especially on your why— the reason you do what you do and the impact you want to make in this world—the better off you're actually going to be.

I have years' worth of data on myself, but you can also read the research around why having one singular focus or far fewer focuses allows you to turn up and do the deeper work and the more meaningful and impactful work.

I can't deny that having lots of things on your plate and lots of ideas and lots of balls in the air is an exciting way to live (especially for Type As and go-getters), but it is not a sustainable one.

YOU NEED TO SPOT BURNOUT BEFORE IT BITES YOU IN THE ASS.

One of the first ways to spot impending burnout is if you are firing on all cylinders, like I had been for months, and feel like you're at the top of your game, like you're nailing everything and you're running at the speed of light. But in fact you're only just barely managing to hold on to all those balls you're juggling in the air.

The second is if you are not sleeping well and your mind is super busy at night, and even with meditation or reading you can't slow it down. This leads to a crappy quality of sleep that only worsens.

The third way to spot burnout is that little things are stressing you more than normal. So you might be reacting strangely or overreacting to something somebody says to you. Or little things might be making you teary or highly emotional, more so than normal. Maybe you're watching a movie and you burst out crying and can't stop.

A fourth way is kind of the flip side of all the above. You might be a little bit too calm about everything that's happening. Like you're zoning out anything because you're just in this do, do, do mode.

Think of it like the calm before the storm. I was noticing that if I wasn't getting overly emotional about stuff (which I wasn't), I was handling everything almost too well, and things that might normally rattle me or upset me felt cruisy.

The reality is that I was not really being honest with how I was feeling and I was keeping a lot of the emotion down and adopting the 'Keep calm and carry on' mantra front and centre. I was thinking and doing, and ignoring *feeling* and *being.*

The fifth way that you can spot burnout is that you are simply not taking any time out for yourself. Every single moment of your day is filled with something. It could be work, sport, catching up with friends, even a 'leisure' activity, but every single moment is filled.

There is zero personal time for you. You are not making time to go and have a massage, to have a nap, even to breathe deeply!

Maybe you've stopped all the fun things that you normally do, like watching your favorite TV series or going out for dinner with the girls. And meditation and/or reading a book in the sunshine—not even on your radar.

HOW TO STOP YOURSELF FROM BURNING OUT

Ultimately it's up to us to look after ourselves and nurture our mind, body, and soul. If we get exhausted, we are now basically crippled by ourselves, by our overly driven nature. What does that mean, exactly?

First, we're no good to ourselves. Second, we are screwing over our friends, our families, and our loved ones. Third, we can't even turn up and serve the people in this world we most want to help.

So it starts with you. It starts with you appreciating yourself first and foremost, and you are your number one priority.

It's like when you're on the airplane and they tell you to put the oxygen mask on yourself first before tending to everybody else. This is the time for you to breathe with that oxygen; take a deep breath, and continue with four to five deep belly breaths, so that you can truly just find some inner peace and calm in between all this *doing*.

I admit that it took me a while to acknowledge that I would only continue to burn out if I didn't stop. It's likely never going to be a good time for you to truly rest up, but it's a damn sight better than being so exhausted that you can't function.

The second time I got close to burnout, ironically right after listening to my friend speak about her experience of it at a conference, I went home and took five days off. I slept a lot, I napped a lot, I read books, I did a lot of nothing.

And guess what? Once I stopped I could barely move. I was that exhausted, that even little decisions felt hard. I took all responsibility off my plate for those five days. I let people know that I wasn't available. I didn't take on any commitments. I barely left the house.

I hung out with my dogs. I sat out in the sun and got my vitamin D. I watched nature. I listened to the birds. I fell asleep on the deck chair. I lay in the grass. I did the least number of things possible.

I was really kind to myself. I took things easy, I did things slowly, and I filled myself with nourishing healthy food, lots of sleep, lots of rest, and hydrated like crazy.

I also soaked up Mother Nature as best I could. I lay in the grass and looked up at the sky, I sat by our gurgling stream and just watched the water. I sat and stared at our trees and listened to the bird song. I did some gentle gardening and slowed the fuck down. This restored my energy and joy levels more than I thought was possible.

I want you to burn bright, my love, not burn out. So take heed of my story, and keep a close eye on you, because you are your most precious asset. Treat yourself like the star you truly are.

PART 4

OPENING YOUR TREASURE CHEST

True wealth comes from valuing what lies within you,
over anything else. It starts with knowing your worth,
understanding your unfair advantage, and appreciating
the abundance that you are entirely capable
of achieving.

BE A LEADING LEARNER, NOT AN EXPERT

If you asked me what really lights me up and what I love to do, I would tell you that I just want to learn all the time. It's my happy place. I love learning and then teaching what I've learned to others. It's something I've always done and always loved.

I have a very distinct memory from when I was age 16, and studying for my final-year school exams. Two of my favourite subjects were art history and classics, and we had the same teacher for both.

I adored Mrs Hawkes. She was the kind of teacher who laughed a lot and made learning fun. She would jump up on a desk and reenact Alexander the Great riding out onto the battlefield. Her style of teaching allowed me to let my imagination run wild, and transport myself back to incredible locations like the Parthenon in Athens in its heyday. The way she taught us all the minute details of a Matisse painting, accompanied by details of his life and personality, brought the artwork to life even more.

I loved learning about the historic figures and creative masters, so when it came to exam times, I turned my bedroom into a wall of images accompanied by sticky notes with key points, facts, and answers that I expected would appear on the exam.

As a visual learner and processor with a somewhat photographic memory, I could actually recall some of these Post-it Note visuals and facts in my exam. But it was what I did with all those notes that really helped me nail my exams (well, most of them).

I used to pace or dance around my bedroom repeating these facts and stories, visualising these humans' daily life in the era they lived. I'd tell embellished stories about these historical figures, and back it up with the notes I had taken to make sure I wasn't talking crap. It was the way that I could actually teach myself by pretending I was teaching someone invisible in the room.

Even if I have the simplest understanding of a concept I've just learned or read about, the easiest way for me to retain this newfound knowledge, and to really understand the context, the philosophy, or the theory behind it, is to share it with others.

Author Richard Bach is famously quoted as saying, *'We teach best what we most need to learn'*. This has always been true for me, in life and in business. I suggest you try this method yourself and see how it works for you. I think you'll surprise yourself.

Back in my 'body sculpting days', which spanned a nine-month period, I got super lean and buff and was so fascinated with the transformation my body was going through from training daily that I wanted to learn more about the amazing human body.

So I took on some extramural study in the evenings, by doing a Certificate in Exercise Prescription from Otago University. I was working full time in a great marketing job back then, plus going to the gym twice a day, seven days a week, so I would literally squeeze this study in around all that.

I remember coming home each night to my boyfriend and flat mates and saying, 'Hey, did you know that we have over 200 bones in our body?' Or 'Most men will lose about 30% of their muscle mass during their lifetimes'. Each night I'd come home and teach them a little something that I learned that day, so that I would instantly retain that information.

Over time, I took it upon myself to teach friends and family, basically anyone and everyone who showed a genuine interest in nutrition, training, and injury prevention. As I was learning I was sharing what I knew, and if I didn't know I'd go and look it up and find out for them. This ultimately meant I learned more once again.

I became quite knowledgeable, perhaps even dangerously so! But I wouldn't give people health advice; I'd give them my opinion on what I was learning and what studies had shown, and what was working for me. People appreciated it. It got them curious, they learned something, I learned even more, and we all walked away knowing more than we did before.

THAT'S WHY I'M A *BIG* FAN OF SHOWING UP AS A LEADING LEARNER, VERSUS BEING LABELED AN EXPERT.

So what's the difference and why can it help you immensely to become a leading learner?

An expert is someone with huge depth of knowledge and understanding of a niche topic that they've studied and applied for years, if not decades. It takes a long time to get this status and is quite the achievement.

A leading learner, however, is you and me: someone who *loves* learning, sharing and applying the results as they learn, and teaching others. In that way you're just a few steps ahead of everyone else, but you're willing to share what you know as you learn it so others can use this valuable information to leapfrog to where you are. It means you don't have to worry about knowing all the answers, or feeling like a fraud or imposter. You just learn, grow, apply, implement, teach—rinse and repeat.

I've gone deep into all sorts of areas and learned amazing skills over the years by showing up as a student first, teacher second. It's served me well enough to be an 'expert' in several areas now—yet I never stop learning or upskilling.

Well, 'never' is a strong word. When I have, I've become complacent in my 'expert' status, and that is dangerous territory. The minute you stop learning, and leading, you stagnate. And like love, learning is all around you. You can learn something every day in every interaction you have in the street, with every person you meet, every video you watch online, every podcast you listen to.

They're all teaching you things, if you're open to it.

Then you can turn around and say to a friend, 'So I was watching this video today on dog training. Did you know that if your dog puts their paw on you, it can be their way of saying "I love you"?'

This doesn't mean you are now an expert in all things dog, but you're able to pass on what you've learned because you've consumed it, shared it, and now are more likely to retain it. Where the real magic comes in is when you can teach it, with your own examples of how you've *applied* what you learned.

If you love learning and you're able to teach it in a way that simplifies it and makes it easy for people to take on board, then you start to love the art of teaching and sharing too. While you may not consider yourself a great teacher, it's a skill that you can work on and continue to improve.

Start by taking something you're curious about, read up about it, aim to understand the concept that you're learning, and then share it in a way that is plain speak— you know, the way that your friends and family can actually understand.

BEING A LEADING LEARNER TAKES A LOT OF PRESSURE OFF YOU.

It means you can turn up and just go with the flow, rather than berate yourself by saying, 'Oh my gosh, I can't teach this, because I'm not an expert.' Or 'Who am I to sell a course on this or [insert excuse here: write a book on this subject, write a blog post on this issue, create a service for my customers on this topic], because I've only been doing it for five months'.

Here's the cold hard truth, lovely. If you've only been doing it that long, and you've been getting great results and seen success from applying what you've learned, then you're already a leading learner.

If you really understand it and you love it and you're passionate about it, then be a leading learner and share your knowledge and steps you took to get your results with other people to help them get up to speed too.

You don't have to be some expert who's strived at this for ten years in order to be able to share something useful and valuable with the person next to you, even if you are literally just a step ahead. That is the whole definition of what being a leading learner is about. This concept has allowed me to build an entire business around what I know and can teach others, through online courses, group coaching, workshops, webinars, live events, my podcast, blog, and videos.

It's my calling. I literally can't stop myself from sharing what I know. And people pay me for it. I may not be the best (almost certainly not), I may not know that much, but I can damn well teach it in a way that people get, grasp, and put into action. That's really valuable to others. Especially since they are all so 'short on time' and seeking shortcuts.

Do not hold back from sharing and teaching others on a topic you have experience and knowledge in, even if it's more recent, just because you don't think you're expert enough. Just turn up as a leading learner. And remember to be a student first and a teacher second. This attitude will benefit you in the long run, and allow you to help tons of people when they need you most.

CHARGE WHAT YOU'RE WORTH

Ah, the million-dollar question, literally and meta-phorically: How do you charge what you're worth?

This is one of my favourite topics to address. It's something that constantly plagues women who are super talented, with a lot of experience, who simply undersell themselves.

Why is charging what you're worth such a big deal? Why do women in particular consistently undervalue themselves and charge way less than they should?

When will we acknowledge that by valuing ourselves, we value others too, and it has a ripple effect in the people we interact with, invest in, and work with?

The way I see it, we have two choices.

> OPTION A: If I earn more, I can spend more, I can pay people more, and I can invest more into others and live a more abundant and fulfilling life.

OPTION B: If I repeatedly undercharge, I develop a scarcity mindset. I don't have money to pay the bills, I become a scrooge, and I do everything on the cheap. I then have less to give to others who need it, and I feel like a constant cheap-ass failure.

I'd choose Option A any freaking day!

Here's an interesting fact. When I was in the nine-to-five world I had no trouble asking to be paid what I was worth, negotiating more money or benefits and walking away if we didn't reach a satisfactory outcome. Once I started my business, however, it took way too long to charge what I was worth and put real value on the work I did.

After one too many 'Can I pick your brain' moments early on in business, I realised I'd helped contribute to people's attitudes of expecting everything for free. I know I'm not alone in this massive oversight, and it took some time to attract genuine people to my community who were willing to pay to access my knowledge, skills, and advice from day one.

If you're not there yet, when you next look at your bank account, or feel sorry for your broke ass, may I suggest you Suck It Up, Princess, and start charging what you're freaking worth!

If you're trapped in fear, doubt, and questions of self-worth, those issues will lead to you undercharging, and that leads to you playing it small, and having a business that doesn't support you or isn't sustainable.

As a result, people who are either better at marketing or promotion or better at summarising what they can do and how they can help you—but not better than you at what they do—they're the ones who get ahead and get paid great money.

I say enough! Every single woman is worth more than she currently thinks she is, and I imagine what she is charging. I believe getting paid what your worth comes down to four things.

1. Confidence

2. Understanding

3. Money mindset

4. Ethics

Let's start with confidence. This is about being really prepared to stand behind your credentials, your experience, and your abilities, whether you are a super expert or just starting out.

When I first started building my online business, I would focus on being a leading learner, someone just a couple of steps ahead of the person I was teaching. I knew I had valuable knowledge to share, and even though I was by no means an expert, I could still help that person to get to where I was by teaching them what I knew.

As I became more advanced and experienced, I continued to see myself as a leading learner, being able to bring both those just starting out as well as those further along the road up to the level they need to be. The closer they are to where I am in knowledge, skills, and experience, the more I am forced to up my game and my skills and continue to grow and learn. It's a win-win situation as you always want to be learning.

I am also a believer in never assuming you're an expert or guru, and instead knowing there's always more to learn, especially from your students. Sure, some people always position themselves as the definitive expert in that space and demand that you wanted to learn from them. That's their prerogative. I wouldn't go near them.

I'd choose someone I liked, and who was generous in sharing their knowledge, and had the confidence to stand behind what they offered and charge accordingly. Confidence is sexy, and it's attractive to others. So even if you haven't necessarily got lots of clients under you, or lots of customers to date, if you know that you can help them to get a result or transformation that's valuable to them, then you've got all you need.

So put your best foot forward, price yourself accordingly, and then make sure you deliver!

UNDERSTANDING

In Launch Your Damn Course Accelerator, the first thing I spend a lot of time teaching my students about is understanding their ideal avatar—their perfect client.

I get them to spend time getting deep into the mind of the person who they would most like to work with and help. This applies to you too—at any stage of your business, this exercise is invaluable and is usually the missing piece if you're struggling to market yourself effectively and close sales.

By doing this through asking questions, listening, and continuing to go deeper and getting into their head, they begin to understand where they're really at:

- What their pain points are

- What they're struggling with most

- What's important to them

- What they're passionate about

- What pisses them off

- What their biggest fear is

You get the picture. No, literally you get the picture— the visual of who this person is, and you know them so intimately that when you go to market your offers, they feel as if you're speaking directly to them.

I've had people say to me many a time, 'Natalie, it's like you spoke directly to me. It's like you know exactly what I was thinking'. Without sounding like a creepy stalker, that's because if I've done my job right, I actually do!

I take this approach with every launch of a new offer, product, course, or idea I have, and it guides everything I do. From my sales page copy, to my imagery, to my messaging and content, so that I speak to and appeal to that one ideal person.

Through this understanding, I am also able to know where my ideal client is at in terms of what's important to them, what they will spend money on, and how much value they place behind the result I'm wanting them to get.

I get to overdeliver on value, and when they start selling their courses, and making three, four, five, or even ten times what they've invested, then I've got a customer for life!

For me, I make the income I desire, and more importantly the impact I desire, as it furthers my mission of helping 1,000 women earn $10,000 a month and creating a ripple effect of more women earning what they're worth.

MONEY MINDSET

The third reason I believe women don't charge what they're worth is their money mindset.

They often link their ability to make money to stories they're holding onto from childhood about what money means or represents to them.

Perhaps you were taught that money doesn't grow on trees, or that rich people are spoilt and selfish. All these influences you had growing up are now determining what you feel and think about money. It's why you may be happy to give away your best work for free, because charging for it doesn't feel right.

Or why you are constantly undercharging for your services because it feels 'icky' or 'weird' or even plain scary to have more money coming in than you've ever had.

The way I see it is this: playing small in this world and undercharging is serving nobody.

- It's underpaying and undervaluing you.

- It's assuming people who want to work with you don't have much to spend.

- It's putting a whole lot of lack and scarcity in place that becomes a self-fulfilling prophecy.

- It's directly harming and impacting not only you, but your loved ones, family, and others.

That last one may not be so apparent. But think of the people who look up to you. If you're consistently in dire financial straits, or poor because of your own actions, what are you saying to them about who they should be?

Not a lot, that's what.

As a kid, thanks to both my parents, I learned the power of saving my money and spending it wisely early on. I also loved having money to spend. I enjoyed seeing my bank account grow, and I liked the freedom it gave me. I had a healthy relationship with money, but I also decided early on I didn't need too much. Often I used to save up all my pocket money and buy Mum flowers because it made her happy, and it made me happy too—way more so than sweets!

And as 'sweet' as that was, it's also a money block in itself. As an adult, when my business earned me more money than I needed, I would spend a lot of the profit on my friends or even strangers by buying their dinners as a surprise, or buying gifts for people I loved. But I didn't really spend it on me! I could happily spend hundreds of thousands investing in property, but I wouldn't spend so generously on myself.

Your money mindset directly affects what you charge people and how you think about your clients and customers.

On a coaching call with my $10K Club members, I found a repeat pattern was coming up with each question around pricing themselves. It went something like this:

'I don't think people can pay that amount. So that's why I'm going to charge less'.

My response is:

- Have you asked them?
- How do you know what they're thinking or what they can afford?

We do a lot of assuming in our lives. Without validating or testing the thought, we say or think, 'Oh, I just don't think I can charge that because nobody will buy it'.

Don't assume that people can't afford what you have.

That's your own money mindset speaking there, not necessarily theirs!

If they're going to get a lot of value out of what you offer, which allows them in turn to do better work, help more people, and raise their rates, then the sky's the limit on what they're prepared to pay you!

People will move heaven and earth to buy something that they really, really want, especially if it's going to give them the result they need. That also incentivises you to put your best work out there too—so it's a win-win.

LET'S BE ETHICAL, SHALL WE?

The fourth reason around charging what you're worth comes down to your values and ethics. Charge what you're worth, and add a bit extra on for good measure (as you're probably still undercharging).

But don't go over the top because you think you have to, or because you see others doing what you do and charging four times as much. Don't charge tens of thousands just because you can, unless that feels really good to you— then go for it. And hopefully you have a philanthropic plan for the excess once you're done investing in yourself and others.

In this case I believe it's best to look at your ideal avatar, and know your target market. If they're high-end real estate investors, then charge a premium, because the results you will get will turn into massive return on investment for them.

If they're just starting out, and are prepared to invest, don't make them have to borrow heavily against a mortgage or go into debt to work with you. Have an offer that's in their price range that helps them get a leg up in their world. Then once they're earning more, and gaining more confidence, they can step up into the next level offering and pay you accordingly.

I've had my fair share of people attempting to charge me what is a decent deposit on a house, for access to a mastermind group or some coaching. While I don't doubt they're worth it, nor do I suggest they do things differently, I just ain't their ideal customer.

I know I could invest that money in property, the share market, crypto, in other peoples' businesses, or in my team, or all of these things, that would lead to a better return on investment than had I paid them, and them alone.

In short, don't take the piss.

YOU CAN'T AFFORD ME

You know that what you offer is valuable. You know the work you do gets real results. And you know that if someone invests in you, they'll earn double, quadruple. or even ten times what they paid you.

So how do you help someone go from 'I'd really like to do this, but I just can't afford this right now' to 'This is exactly what I need and I'm prepared to pay for it because I know this is totally worth it!'

Let me be clear here. I'm not talking about something that costs less than hundred dollars here—heck no. I'm talking about higher-value offers like a VIP day that's $5,000 or a coaching program over six months that's worth $15,000, for example.

First off, you get really curious when someone says that to you. Get really curious about that statement and then ask questions in a way that allows for their mind to come up with the solution or the answer they need.

Ask them questions:

When you say you can't afford it yet, is it more about making the full payment up front? And if I could offer you a payment plan, would that make it more feasible?

In that moment, you're offering them an option to see that it's possible to do this and to afford it.

Then you say, 'And if I did it, would you be interested?' What you're offering is wiggle room.

If the person responds, 'Look, I would hire you in an instant, but I can't even pay my rent'. Well then, they're right. They can't afford you. And they shouldn't hire you if they can't pay their rent or make their mortgage payment or buy groceries for their family.

If the fact of the matter is that they really don't have the money, then that's okay. Give them your love, send them your blessings, and wish them well.

However, if there is a bit of wiggle room, often you'll have people respond to say, 'Actually I could pay this amount now, and this amount in two weeks'.

Great. Now you have a solution, and you get to work with them, and they get the help they need and deserve. If they really want it enough, they'll do what they can to make it happen.

Now, I can hear you asking, 'Natalie, how much flexibility do you allow in this case, before it starts getting difficult to handle, or it crosses my boundaries?'

I'd suggest asking for a decent chunk of money up front, especially if it's for an event or a service. A great move is 50% up front, and then split the other 50% into two payments. Or you can offer prepayments before they get to work with you. Let's say they do this over three months, and then you start your coaching with them. You'll often find that they will change their mind and pay you in full on the spot, especially if they're keen to work with you straightaway.

Learn from my mistake though. In my generosity one year, I offered a pay-in-full or payment plan for my Freedom Retreat in Bali. For some reason, I structured the payment plan past the actual retreat. This was a $4,000 all-inclusive event, and it was magical.

However, two people skipped out on the last few payments, despite getting a ton of value out of it. They actually ghosted me on my follow-up emails. I was left disappointed and I felt like I got taken advantage of. One of them followed up ages later telling me they'd gone bankrupt before the retreat and were too ashamed to own up.

It was a good lesson learned. So don't do that!

Never be afraid to invite somebody to the next step with you. Because often people won't make a conscious decision to hire you or to buy from you until you invite them. But know that it's okay if they say no; don't freak out about that.

Simply dip your toe in the water and invite somebody. If you're not sure how to phrase it, an easy way is to say, 'You know, I would love to work with you. And if there's ever an opportunity for that to happen, let's talk about it'. Often, planting that seed allows for somebody to realise, 'Oh my gosh, you'd like to work with me? I'd love that. What would that look like? Let's talk about it some more'.

That gives you the opportunity to move on to discovering what that looks like, and often allows you to invent the next-level offer in your business you'd been planning to put out there!

Never be afraid to put an invite out, and never take things personally. Remember, when someone rejects that offer or invite, they're not rejecting you. They're rejecting the thing, because it's not right for them at the time or they're not ready for it yet.

You, however, are born ready. You got this. You're totally worth it!

THE PRICE IS RIGHT

If you're a freelancer or in business for yourself, charging what you're worth may seem scary at first, but once you take that first step, it makes all the fear and trepidation worthwhile—especially once you see a healthy bank balance and rising profits. All it takes is an honest form of communication with existing and new clients on why you're raising your prices, and what that allows you to do.

I once got an awesome email from my web designer at the time, who raised her prices and shared exactly where that money was going to go:

First, to herself, so she could undertake more certification-level training, improve her skills, and give her clients even better results

Second, to hire a team member, so she could serve even more clients, while still upholding the excellent standards she was currently serving her clients

Third, to buy better equipment and tools from which to offer an even higher standard of work

Fourth, to improved servers so her clients would benefit from faster-loading websites, better response time, and countless other benefits

She listed a few more things and then shared some killer results she'd been getting for her clients by way of example of why she was worth it, but honestly she had me at hello!

LISTEN TO THOSE GOLD NUGGETS.

There's a lot of psychology and research around charging more money for what you provide. I've experienced it myself. When you have a higher-price offer, typically people who invest in it also commit more. (Not always, though. Some people will just throw money at things and think that by buying a course, for example, through some magical process they will suddenly be better off, which always baffles me. Why would you invest that much if you're not prepared to do the work?)

But this psychology often works. As you start to raise your prices, you'll find you get a more committed level of client or student, somebody who's prepared to go all in because they put money on the line. And guess what? They're then more likely to get a better result out of it too!

Remember to factor in and account for the years of experience you have, the unique skills and capabilities you bring to the table, the money you've invested in yourself, and then charge appropriately!

HOW DO YOU KNOW WHAT'S APPROPRIATE?

People will tell you very quickly.

If you've priced too low, and it's the right offer, product, or service, people will snap it up, and also tell you it's too cheap.

If you're charging a fair, honest price worthy of your awesomeness, then you'll find a beautiful ease and grace in attracting customers.

If you're too expensive, people will tell you that too. I don't mean just one person saying, 'Gosh you're three times as much as so and so', but you'll find a decent number of people saying the same thing.

If you're launching an online course, for example, you can start with an entry-level price that you're comfortable charging, and that you think people are going to go for. It's going to be a no-brainer price, but you make it very clear that in the future, it's going to be worth a lot more.

When I started out with the Freedom Plan course, I offered it at $497 for the first 30 people in the pilot program. Those 30 spots got filled up in less than three weeks with no marketing outside of a small subset of my list, so I knew I was onto something that people really valued.

When I launched the next round of the full program, I started with an early bird pricing where people could jump on board for 48 hours before it went up to the regular price. This was a $300 saving.

That also helps you test the market. If a bunch of people buy at your early bird price and then you put it up to full price, you'll find that sweet spot where you get the right number of clients or students at a price that feels good to them and to you.

And if there's no natural drop-off at the full price and sales continue to grow, then you know that you can probably charge even more next time. Then, as you continue to launch and improve your offering or course, you can definitely put up your prices to reflect the increased value. It's all about iterating.

Then there'll be a point where you potentially go past what is feasible, or what is market value. Even if your cost is really good, you might just find 'Oh, okay, I've maybe hit that price ceiling'. What's actually happened is that you have often hit your customer ceiling, and you need to move into another profile of clients at the next level.

For example, one of my lovely $10K Club members is a therapist who does amazing work. Yet as she shifted her money mindset in our group and through doing the work in my lessons and coaching, she started finding a lot more people were saying they'd love to work with her, but they can't quite afford her price. She mentioned she's at the higher end of what people were paying for a therapist. Then I showed her an example of another lady, in the same area of therapy she is in, who's charging four to five times as much, and getting a lot of clients.

Why? This lady is not dealing with people who are struggling in life and in their finances; she's dealing with go-getters, successful people who are still struggling with the same issues, but they've got the money and are prepared to invest to deal with what's really hampering them.

I suggested she look at shifting her avatar to those who are further ahead and can afford her. Then she can offer scholarships or pro bono work to those who can't afford her but with whom she still likes to work. By charging appropriately, she's able to help those who pay her what she's worth, and still be able to lift up her other clients.

Remember, the more you grow and step up, the more you lift up those who work with you too.

VALUE YOUR GORGEOUS SELF

I'll never forget the time a friend at work came to see me before she was due to go into a performance review with our general manager.

Kat was an amazing hair technician and a true asset to the company. Even though she was young, she was really skilled and our team of sales reps loved her. The thing is, even though she was being underpaid, she was scared to go and ask for more because she really loved her job and didn't want to do anything to rock the boat.

She came into my office and asked for advice. Even back then I was keen on empowering women to go after their dreams and get what they wanted.

She'd found out that one of our major competitors in the professional haircare industry, L'Oréal, had a job opening for a similar role to the one she was in. Get this though: they were paying $25,000 more than she was currently getting, and it came with a company car and a bonus!

We discussed where she was currently with pay level, what she felt she was worth, and what she really wanted to earn. In essence, we explored what would make her feel like her contribution to the company was valued, make her want to keep doing an amazing job, and continue to grow with the company.

Once we got clear on that, I told her that she should double that amount, and use it as a negotiation tool to land on what she really wanted. She was shocked, but open to trusting me.

We then wrote up a list of her accomplishments to date, and the results she'd been instrumental in getting. We looked at her job description and the tasks she was hired for, and then added all the other things she'd been doing, and had taken on, or had the initiative to start, since she'd been in the role. And again we linked this back to the results she'd accomplished.

I made sure she felt confident and comfortable in what she was going to ask for, and truly believed she deserved it. She was brimming with excitement and nerves, but to her credit, she was ready. With a swish of her gorgeous, healthy, long brown locks, she waltzed out of my small office and directly into the GM's for her review meeting.

Less than 20 minutes later, I heard the door open, she glided out, and knocked on my door. When I beckoned her in, her face was glowing. She squealed in delight: Craig, the GM, had not only met her requests, but given her more than she asked, to sweeten the deal. She gave me a huge hug and skipped off down the hallway.

A few minutes later there was another knock on my door. It was Craig, who asked me to come into his office for a minute.

My heart was beating very fast as I tried to figure out what this was about. I sat down in a comfy chair and turned to meet his gaze.

'So, you probably know that I just gave Kat a massive pay rise.'

'Ah yes, she did just mention that'.

'Yes, and it's well deserved. The thing is, Nat, the walls here are pretty thin, and I could hear your entire conversation, so I guess it's thanks to you that she's getting it. Just don't expect the same result for your performance review, or we'll go out of business with these big increases to our bottom line!'

He said that last part with a twinkle in his eye, and when my review came around, I did get an increase too. Deep down, I think he admired how Kat and I had both approached it, and that we had the lady balls to ask for exactly what we wanted.

If you're in a job you love but are underpaid, how can you apply the above steps to get paid what you feel you're worth and what you deserve?

PART 5

QUEEN OF HEARTS

Self-love is the most beautiful and effective tool we have, to truly step into our Queen power. Once we love ourselves, we can truly love others, unconditionally.

HERE'S TO SELF-LOVE

'You yourself, as much as anybody in the entire universe, deserve your love and affection'.

—BUDDHA

I truly believe that the Beatles got it right when they sang, 'Love is all you need'.

I want you to start a healthy dialogue with yourself on the topics of self-love, also often interchanged with self-worth, so I figured I'd start with sharing a personal story on my journey.

Think about the catchy marketing tagline from cosmetics powerhouse L'Oréal: 'Because you're worth it'.

I used to love hearing this on every ad they played back in the '80s and '90s, especially as a young, impressionable kid and then as a teenager. They still use it to this day, and for good reason! In just four words: 'Because you're worth it', they made me believe in myself. They convinced me, as a woman, that no matter what, I was worth it. Even better, I didn't have to buy their products to feel that way.

I've had a pretty healthy sense of myself and my self-worth for decades. This was definitely helped by my parents' love and positive language, highlighting what I did well and what I was capable of, but particularly by Dad's constant reinforcement: 'Nat, you can do anything you want to in life, and be whoever you want to be, even the prime minister of New Zealand'.

This was further reinforced by the fact that New Zealand was the first country in the world to give women the right to vote, back in 1893, thanks to the efforts of suffrage campaigners, led by Kate Sheppard for three years in a row.

Growing up, I was privileged to have not one but two female prime ministers as role models in Dame Helen Clark and Dr Jenny Shipley. During the same period we had a longstanding female governor general in Dame Catherine Tizard, as well as Teresa Gattung, who was the first woman to run a large New Zealand public company, Telecom, for eight years.

I was surrounded by amazing women, doing incredibly important jobs for our country. All this whilst attending an all-female school, Samuel Marsden Collegiate, renowned for their academic excellence, with an elegant, poised, and kind principal, Miss Button, who taught us the power of studying smart to achieve amazing results, as well as being an all-rounder in sports, arts, and culture. I freaking loved my time there, and my school blazer attested to how much I threw myself into everything, with a plethora of badges for things I was involved with at school.

So yeah, I felt women had the right, the capability, and the power to do and be whatever the heck they wanted.

Once I started travelling the world, I fully appreciated the privilege I grew up in, and that this was definitely not the norm. But it's stuck with me, and always will. Because, damn it, we *are* worth it. And it's up to us to use that to our advantage, and also to nurture ourselves every day, to ensure we can continue to operate from that place of deep and grateful love and acceptance of ourselves.

I took this healthy sense of self-worth and self-love with me into university, and the part-time jobs I got during my study to ensure I had an income, a sense of responsibility, and a strong foundation on which to launch into my career once I finished my two bachelor's degrees.

One of these jobs was modelling, an industry that I knew, even at the young age of 16, was responsible for a lot of serious mental and physical health issues in young women. I saw my fair share of waiflike girls, looking miserable and being extremely self-conscious, with a strong attitude of self-loathing toward themselves.

When I started modelling, the days of curvy, strong, and healthy role models like Cindy Crawford were making way for the gothic, drug-addicted, translucent, looks-more-like-a-teenage-boy type of model. It wasn't a look I could ever achieve, nor one I even remotely wanted to resemble. There were times I was told I needed to lose some weight or do certain things to look a certain way and fit in. But I never succumbed, and I never envisaged modelling as my chosen career path.

Ironically, modelling—which could easily have depreciated my sense of self-worth and self-esteem—only heightened it. Despite being told I wasn't the look *du jour,* despite coming second place in the 'Face of 95' back when I first started, despite being told to be thinner, less 'girl next door' in my look, I honoured myself. I used who I was to find a niche within which people appreciated me for myself.

That niche happened to be in lingerie modelling. If you ever want to learn to love your body more, or accept it as it is, as well as draw on your inner confidence and love, try walking around in sexy lingerie on catwalks, or in front of department store buyers scrutinising every aspect of what you're wearing—which can feel exactly like they're scrutinising you!

Modelling lingerie was the first time I discovered I had boobs. Before then I thought mine were pretty tiny, but turns out my breasts were a healthy size. And my natural curves and the butt that has always stuck out saying 'Look at me!' is something that looks hot in lingerie. Who knew? Certainly not my young, naive, teenage self.

Even better, compared to my fellow student friends getting around $8–10 per hour, I was getting paid NZ

$120 for a two-hour minimum (beyond any students' wildest dreams) often for only 30 minutes of work. What's more, I was standing around in beautiful Bendon lingerie, in front of a few department store buyers who were extremely respectful, usually women, and always complimentary to me and the lingerie.

AN EXAMPLE OF SELF-LOVE IN ACTION

I'm not saying over the years I haven't wished for skinnier legs or a smaller butt or a whole lot of things to be different, but most of the time I am beyond thankful for my German and English heritage that gives me height, strong bones, athletic prowess, and delicious curves.

I regularly share gratitudes with my body and my mind for getting me through a triathlon, or powering me through a strength routine, or for showing up daily in yoga with grace, poise, and suppleness. I honour my body for having the ability to do handstands, cartwheels, and round-offs that I learned in my short stint in gymnastics as a kid, and found I can still do almost as effortlessly. The fact I can even do them at all makes my heart sing.

This body has seen me through hundreds of games of Ultimate Frisbee, and many layouts—when you dive in the air for a disc and land on the ground, fully outstretched, hopefully with the disc still in hand. It's seen me through too many knee-jarring and ankle-rolling games of netball and tennis, and of course through all my cycling events and triathlons, as well as 6,500km of cycling through Africa. And even the bone- and intestine-jarring motocross races, from my late teens to early 20s, where I did some magnificent yet unintentional aerial dismounts and not so brilliant full-throttle crashes.

All of this desire to push and grow myself has resulted in just one broken wrist, and a whole heap of adrenalin, fun, challenge, and a never-ending appreciation of the incredible natural machines our bodies truly are. The fact that our heart beats about 100,000 times a day and about 35 million times in our lifetime is reason to have gratitude, respect, and a massive dose of self-love for yourself, isn't it?

You are an amazing human, love on you!

In the next chapter I'll share more on how to do that.

DOSE UP ON YOUR SELF-WORTH

One of the most precious commodities you have is self-respect, which starts with you, and then leads to others respecting you too.

First off, you need to realise that your self-worth and value are not tied to what you do, but to who you are. That's what really matters. No matter whether you win awards or accolades for your performance, you still can have the same high opinion of your *value* as a person.

To do this, remind yourself that your bank account, job title, attractiveness, and social media following have nothing to do with how valuable or worthy a person you are.

What society tells us we should value—things like money, status, and popularity—aren't what you necessarily value deep down in yourself in others. The traits I seek out in friends and other people I admire are values like kindness, compassion, respect for others, empathy, and treating people well.

I believe every one of us needs to learn to love ourselves, and that is much easier to do when we show ourselves some self-compassion. I know I'm the least self-compassionate with myself when I'm wanting to control outcomes and all the moving parts of my life and business.

- It's not letting up on myself and always expecting more.

- It's not stopping to actually check in with how I *feel*.

- It's using passion and purpose as an excuse, not to pause and reflect.

When I get really honest with myself, I'd love to reduce my tendencies to feel like I have to strive in order to achieve, or go at a million miles an hour. I know I need to stop holding all the to-dos and priorities in my mind, stop taking on more responsibilities, and stop skipping regular digital detoxes!

That's where the practice of self-compassion has amplified my attitude of kindness toward myself and others, my ability to be present and at peace, my inner calmness and love, and my capability to practice nonjudgement—this is huge.

So how do I practice more self-compassion?

- Daily rituals that allow me to focus on the present, including gratitudes, yoga, meditation, and journaling

- Taking quality time out in nature, especially the forest with my beautiful dogs

- Enjoying twice-monthly pampering sessions like a massage, float tank, or spa experience

- Celebrating the small and big wins regularly, and acknowledging when I've done great work, or been a good friend, loving partner, or fab fur baby mum.

HOW ELSE CAN YOU INCREASE YOUR SELF-LOVE AND COMPASSION FOR YOURSELF?

Fall in love with yourself, love yourself first, then true love will come to you.

Self-praise boosts your self-esteem. Criticism withers it. So instead of criticising yourself, praise yourself on a regular basis. Look in the mirror and say, 'Dang Princess, you are looking stunning today, and you are positively glowing!'

Write phrases on your mirror: I am lovable. I am amazing. I am worthy. I matter. I am a great person.

Do your daily gratitudes, even on the days when the most you can muster is that you're grateful you woke up! From there more reasons for gratefulness will flow, and soon you'll be in a much more abundant and joyful place.

It really works. If you do this every day, your mind starts to believe it. And it starts to sink in. Your choice is to choose to praise you. Then you can access this new belief and say goodbye to your inner critic, your fear, your imposter syndrome, your ego, and say hello to loving you.

BREAK UP WITH YOUR BAD ROMANCE

I'm not gonna lie to you, when I was a kid I often bought into the fairy-tale romance that I was exposed to over and over in movies, books, and, well, fairy tales. The perfect guy was out there and our life would be perfect together. At least that's what I thought when I fell madly in love with my first boyfriend at the ripe age of 20.

Before that, I'd been too focused on school and sport even to be interested in boys. I remember a playground game we played sometimes at school when I was young, where the boys would chase the girls. If one of them caught you, he got to lift your skirt up and take a sneak peek at your panties. Yep, sexist as heck. And yet most of the girls 'let' themselves be caught. Not me—I freaking ran as fast as I could, determined to win and never be caught.

That independent and competitive streak was ingrained in me from a young age. I grew up with a strong sense of what was possible, on my own terms and of my own volition.

So why was it that in my first relationship I chose to fall for a villain, rather than my Prince Charming? How did this confident, self-assured, independent, well-adjusted young woman fall in love with a guy 15 years her senior, who had massive insecurity and trust issues, and stay in a relationship with him for four years?

This seemingly charming, funny man turned out to be emotionally abusive, and once he even hit me in a moment of anger, for which I never forgave him.

The first year was a beautiful, addictive romance of hot sex, some drugs, and alcohol (he owned a restaurant and his friends owned bars...what can I say?). I had found a bad boy and soon realised that came with a 'bad love'. He was so hung up on his alcoholic mother's past indiscretions, including leaving his dad for his best friend, that he already had it against us from the get-go. He simply couldn't stop blaming everyone else for who he'd become, and why he was the way he was.

I stepped in to 'save' him and show him what a great, stable relationship with love and respect could be, and modelling the 'normal' and happy family life I'd been privileged to grow up in. And he did everything in his power to show me that was never going to happen, despite the fact that I knew he genuinely loved me.

There were two defining moments that made me realise what a fool I'd been, and that things were never going to change. The first was my friend Lisa coming back from England and spending a day out with us. After a car ride into town, she gently pulled me aside and asked me how the heck I let him talk to me like that.

'Like what?' I asked, genuinely curious.

'He just swore at you when you were driving and put you down several times; didn't you hear that? No one deserves to ever talk to my Nat like that'.

I was stunned. I hadn't heard that at all. The truth was, for self-preservation, I had gotten really good at tuning out the emotional abuse, in order to keep the peace and enjoy the good times in between the drama. But she was right. Who the heck was I ever to let *anyone* speak to me like that, let alone someone I loved and who loved me.

I thanked her for the wakeup call. She still looked shocked as we headed off to dinner.

The second moment that reality truly hit home was listening to my dear friend Cindy, the office manager at one of my part-time jobs I had during university. She'd become a great friend and confidant. She knew my boyfriend (our boss was a friend of his), and she'd witnessed all our ups and downs just by observing me at work, and when he came in to visit.

On this particular day, I'd phoned him up with some happy news about my day at university and what I'd learned, only to be completely beaten down by his pessimistic and sarcastic response.

I got off the phone teary, and yet again baffled by the amount of sheer hurt he could cause me in an instant. Cindy looked at me compassionately and said, 'Ohhhh Nat, one day you will wake up and realise what a complete loser he is, and that you are an amazing woman meant for so much more, and someone who loves you unconditionally'.

I stopped in my tracks, and finally took it all in. This was probably the fortieth time Cindy had said something in a similar vein, but this time I was truly listening and my rose-tinted glasses were no longer blinding me.

I couldn't believe what a fool I had been to ignore all my good friends, who'd been enduring my drama and this shitty relationship, giving me truly solid advice again and again, only to watch me walk right back into the thick of it. What a sucker for punishment I was.

So I took action. I want to share the steps I intuitively took to reclaim my life and sense of self.

REDRAW YOUR BOUNDARIES

Even before I finally realised this was not the type of relationship I ever envisaged being in, I had been summoning up the courage to start making a life outside of 'us' and building up a fortress of friends, networks, and other interests.

This turned out to be the smartest thing I ever did, over the space of almost a year. It meant I had a complete safety net and new life that already existed, once I was single again.

Boundaries are an essential part of practicing love with yourself and others. It's a key time to build your own moat around you, Warrior Princess.

Make sure you read the Build Your Moat Chapter.

FORGIVE YOURSELF

I can't tell you how many nights I lay awake in bed wondering what the fuck I was doing, and how stupid I had been. I berated myself for even getting into this relationship the first place, and even thought that perhaps I deserved his abuse.

What an abuser does to you is wrong. You never deserved it. The guilt, shame, and fear you experience are not yours to own. The thing you need to give yourself most, and what you deserve more than ever, is self-forgiveness and self-compassion.

The more I rationally thought through the situation I'd put myself in, the more I realised I was a loving person who deserved none of this crap and that I needed to support myself 100% right now.

The more I reached out to friends and peers to talk about how I was feeling, directly or indirectly, the more I realised how I was not to blame, and their perspectives helped me regain a sense of normalcy in my life, and to focus on thoughts about what was right and what was wrong in love and in life.

TAKE YOUR TIME

Less than a week after that conversation with my friend Cindy, I was more than ready to walk away and get on with my life.

I got back from university and packed up the last of my stuff at his house, put it in the car, then wandered out the back to see him sitting in the spa—my spa—and I simply said, 'Hey'.

He looked up and gave me a grunt as a hello. I fully realised in that moment I gave zero fucks about him anymore. I felt so liberated. I was finally free. I saw him through crystal-clear eyes that revealed to me a person I no longer knew, loved, or cared for, but wasn't inherently a bad person. He was just a wounded soul, and not my soul to heal.

Without any emotion, I said, 'Goodbye, Kurt, I'm leaving you. I genuinely wish you happiness in life'.

He didn't initially look at me, and no doubt thought this was yet another break-up argument. I stood silently and then he looked up at me said, 'Yeah, whatever'.

I smiled, turned, and walked away. And I never looked back.

For you, the sooner you get out the better. But know that your abuser wants you to feel lost, scared, and alone, and when you leave them it may feel like there's a massive hole in your life without them.

For me, I felt the opposite for many weeks, but then it's easy to reflect on the good or great times and forget the reality of what you had.

Your life is your own to live, and you can take as much time as you want and need to recover and rediscover you. Remember, there is no time limit on healing. And while I didn't go to therapy, if I'd known more about it at that young age, and it was more accessible like it is now, I would have totally taken it.

USE YOUR POWER

What ensued after I left him was a broken-hearted man, not at all ready to accept that I was no longer in his life. I won't bore you with the details, only to share that the only time I've ever walked into a police station in my life was to ask for help with how to stop an ex-boyfriend from harassing and threatening me by phone and texts.

Thankfully, they took calm and decisive action and I never heard from him again, until around 15 years later, when he rang to apologise.

But in those first few months after I left him, trying to make sense of the abuse and how to feel now felt like a tough ask on some days and almost impossible on bad ones. Luckily, I had dear friends and family around me, who I'd had honest conversations with, or who'd witnessed the bad love, and were honouring the boundaries I'd put in place.

In that year while I was building up the courage to leave him, they kept me strong when I was weak, and helped me to see the path that I was on was the right one. They provided counsel and guidance when I left to make sure I never returned, and while most of it was my own inner knowing and strength, I am so grateful for their support.

You have all the power you need at your fingertips— internet searches will reveal workshops, therapists, counsellors, courses, and events to help you heal and evolve.

Make sure you use all of them to become the Queen you truly are.

I see you. I love you. Now love yourself and set yourself free.

TAKE A CHANCE ON LOVE

I'm wandering through LAX airport, with an hour to enjoy before my flight to Cuba boards. The airport is bustling, every person with their own agenda, place to be or go. I'm meandering slowly, lost in my thoughts.

On the one hand, I'm excited to be visiting Cuba for the first time, and I was excited about the man I was going with. At least I was up until about a week ago, when I'd met another man and we'd both fallen for each other—fast.

'How did this all happen?' I asked myself.

You see, back in 2009 when I was living in Vancouver and was very new to my role as co-founder of a tech business, I knew I needed some help and guidance. So I'd joined the women's mentor network and been matched with one of the few male mentors, because he also had a tech company.

The day I walked into his office for our first official mentor hour I was impressed. He was charming, handsome, and successful. He was also calm, gave great advice, and had years of experience in growing his company.

After several mentor meetings, he invited me to a fancy black-tie party in Vancouver, and who I was to resist? We loosely agreed that this was not a date and would be great for networking.

But who were we kidding? I went for pre-event drinks at his lovely apartment. He looked great in his tuxedo, and then we were whisked away in a private car to this fundraising event.

Vancouver is filled with beautiful people, and this particular party had scooped up the crème de la crème. These also happened to be very well connected and wealthy people, and I was just along for the ride.

The champagne flowed, the music wafted over us, and the night became intoxicating. Several hours in, Mr Mentor and I had shifted into some serious line crossing by dancing and making out. It all felt surreal, especially for a struggling startup entrepreneur who was renting with friends, cycling to work, and living on a small budget.

The next day, I was flying to the US to spend time with a guy I'd met around five months back. The timing of this new 'romance' was ironic, to say the least. You see, back around the July 4th weekend, I'd driven with my teammates to Redmond, Washington, to play in a legendary Ultimate Frisbee tournament I'd always wanted to go to. We found ourselves at one of the biggest social yet competitive mixed tournaments in the US. Hundreds of athletes were everywhere, and spread out across the multitude of grass fields just waiting for some disc action.

I was in heaven as I got set to play with my Vancouver team of friends in a raucous, fun-filled three days, complete with teams playing high-level Ultimate Frisbee in costumes, with camping and all-night parties. It's the perfect recipe for good times, hilarity, and fun flings. Trust me, you just have to be there to understand the special kind of event this is.

On the very last day of the tournament, while having drinks with my team and new friends and watching the final of an incredible game of what is basically Canada versus USA mixed national teams, I meet 'the other guy'.

In a moment of sunshine, exhaustion from playing so many games, lack of sleep from partying hard, the cider I was drinking, and the banter going on from the sidelines, we bumped into each other in a most unexpected way.

A kissing game had broken out (yep, that's Ultimate Frisbee players for you) and my dear friend Alyssa was in the thick of it. She somehow pulled me in and the guy in question dared her to kiss me, which she did. Then she dared him to do the same to her, then me...you know the game.

Trouble is he was a damn good kisser and there was an electricity between us that couldn't be denied.

'Why did we meet on the very last day, just 30 minutes before the teams were heading home?' we lamented to each other. We exchanged phone numbers and he made some grand sweeping statement about coming to hang with him in Manhattan Beach.

Which leads me to why I'm at LAX, six months later, heading to Cuba to meet my mentor, who's seven years older than me, single, successful, and accomplished, and who is flying out from Vancouver to join me. But I'm secretly wanting to stay on and go back to 'the other guy', who is around seven years younger, care-free, not really working, still studying, and a someone I just spent a whirlwind fun few days with.

I know, this doesn't sound like a tough predicament at all—kind of a win-win either way. But something in my gut is thinking that I should follow my instincts and make the most of this new romance, which totally caught both of us off guard.

Then my phone rings, and my hunch is validated. It's Mr Mentor saying his granny, whom he adores and told me he adored from the first minute I met him, has fallen ill and he doesn't feel right leaving her just before New Year's.

Listening to him tell me this, I'm kind of stunned. His parting words: 'I'm so sorry. I know this isn't ideal, but you must still go to Cuba and have a blast. Everything is booked. So enjoy'. I'm still not sure to this day whether that was legit or an excuse, but who cares!

When we hung up, I took all of three seconds to decide that I was not going to go to Cuba. I was going to spend New Year's Eve with my new lover.

I called him and said, 'Hey, it's me. I've got good news and bad news'.

Him: 'Oh wow, do tell'.

Me: 'The bad news is, I'm not going to Cuba. The good news is, I can come spend New Year's with you'.

Granted, I hadn't thought this through at all. I just assumed that he'd be thrilled at this news, and luckily he was.

He said, 'I'm turning the car around and coming back to pick you up!'

I was elated. I ran up to the agent at the boarding gate and asked if it was possible to get my bag off this flight and not be on it. She was pretty stunned but somehow made it happen.

I made my way back through security, getting odd looks from the LAX staff, and out the other side to be picked up by my lover, and spent an entirely wild and awesome New Year's together that I'll never forget.

The entire point of this story is that being a free-spirited young woman is one of the biggest gifts we are given. I chose to use this time to make some of the best decisions in the moment, based on what my heart and gut were telling me. It felt truly liberating, empowering, and amazing.

And I continued to follow the advice from both my heart and gut for years to come, especially once I became a footloose and fancy-free full-time world traveller and entrepreneur. One day, you and I can sit down over a glass of bubbles, wine, or Kombucha, because I have a lot more stories like that to share.

So where can you show up fully, in your beautiful playful Princess mode, and take a chance on love?

FIND YOUR PRINCE OR PRINCESS CHARMING

My journey to finding my Prince, nay King was not a straightforward one. As a kid, I had bought into those fairy-tale movie romances a little too much. Now, as an adult I was often disappointed by the 'real' deal.

I do, however, believe in a love story built on mutual respect, trust, adoration, and the core values you hold dearest.

I also believe that you are worthy of a love that befits a Queen—whether you wish for a Prince, a King, a Queen, a Jester, or whoever the heck you wish to love, and be loved by.

I've been in three main relationships. The first felt like a rendition of meeting the big bad wolf. The second, while lovely, felt like the porridge was not too hot, too cold, or just right; it was simply too independent.

The third—well so far, looking at the mirror, mirror on the

wall—it's looking great. And it's this one that I'd like to share the story of.

It all started after six years of singledom, international romances, and flings on my travels. I arrived home in New Zealand in late 2015 to be with my dad, who'd gotten very sick, very quickly.

After we lost him in December that year, I felt that perhaps it was time to stop telling everyone, 'I love being single, and couldn't be happier', when deep down I questioned if that was still true.

Losing my dad, one of the most honourable, loveable, kind, gentle, and beautiful men I knew, had made me want someone special in my life, not as a replacement, but to further my belief that men like him did in fact exist out there in the world.

THE PERFECT 'PERSON' LIST

It was around this time, in January 2016, that my friend Davina suggested I write a 'Perfect Man list'.

'A what?' I asked, genuinely perplexed.

'You know, a definitive list of all the traits and qualities you wish in your perfect man. Be as specific as you can be and just let rip. I suggest you start writing and keep writing until you can't think of anymore'.

We did this one night over dinner, after she convinced me it was how she met her amazing man, now her husband and the father of their kids.

Considering that I made all my clients and Freedom Plan members write their perfect day, and knowing how stunningly effective this form of visualisation and getting clear on what you want could be, I started writing.

Ten things on my list later, I was struggling.

Davina looked over my shoulder and said, 'That's a great start, but list everything. Like do you want them to get on with your mother? Do you want them to have good teeth? Can they dance well?'

I wrote some more. I had instinctively listed values like integrity and honesty first, then qualities like emotional intelligence, a sense of adventure, and a great sense of humour.

What made me squirm was focusing on the physical aspects, because deep down I knew that if they had the qualities I desired, and our values aligned, it really didn't matter how attractive they were. I would be attracted to those things already, and if they were tall, dark, and handsome, then bonus!

'Okay, I think I'm done', I announced hopefully. She looked it over and said, 'Eighteen things on your list is good, but aim for 100, or at least 50. Get really clear on your "perfect" partner. Trust me on this'.

I needed more wine!

We got the giggles as she shared some of the ones she put on her list, and then I got it. Write *everything* down. Everything you long for, wish for, desire, and more. It's not about being greedy or fanciful; it's about telling the universe, 'Hey, this is the exact person I'd like to meet and love. Please send them my way, or anyone who nearly fits the bill'.

The next step was to put this list away in a drawer, refer to it every so often, and read over it. But basically let the universe do its thing.

The other step I knew I needed to take was to start telling myself and others the truth.

Each time I caught up with a friend who knew I was back in town, after being away for ten or more years, or meeting new friends or entrepreneurs, when they asked a question related to love I'd answer, 'I'm loving life, and I'm always open to meeting someone fabulous to share it with'.

This sentence in itself made me initially want to cringe! Then the more I said it, the more I believed it, and allowed it to be true—because it was true.

Less than a month later I was attending an amazing event called New Frontiers. It ran over four days but I could only attend one. Speaking on that day was a rather intriguing man. As he took the stage to talk about a topic that was far over my head (and the heads of many others), I was drawn to this super-intelligent being who looked part hippy, part uncomfortable, and at the same time commanded presence and respect.

What an intoxicating combination, I thought to myself.

After his talk, I had to leave, so I wandered over shyly (surprised at my shyness) to thank him for his talk. This romantic fairy-tale moment went something like this:

Me: 'Hi Josh. I'm Natalie. Thanks so much for that fascinating talk. I really enjoyed it'.

Him: 'Hello'.

Me: 'I've got to go now. Bye'.

Him: 'Okay, bye. Thanks for coming over'.

I smiled, turned, and walked off. I did genuinely have to go, but once in his presence, I also felt that I really shouldn't take up more time than needed, and there were a lot of people waiting to talk to him.

Strike forward to April and I was asking friends about who would be best to speak to about my Right to Freedom Project, and this man's name came up several times.

So I bit the bullet, emailed him after looking him up

online, again bemused by his mix of curly hair, glasses, and geeky demeanour and the yet spiritualness of his profile. I didn't really expect a response because somehow I had pegged him as too busy or too important to answer his emails.

Not long after, I sent a short email:

> Hi Josh.
>
> We met at New Frontiers. I hear you're the man about town to talk to about freedom. Would you be open to meeting up to discuss a project I'm working on? Thanks
>
> Natalie

I received a reply within minutes.

> Yes. When and where?
>
> JV

Ha, that was easier than I thought. A few days later we met at Olive Cafe. As I walked in and saw him, my heart skipped a bit.

Damn, I felt attracted to him. Play it cool, Nat, this is a business meeting.

He apparently thought the same, and for the hour we

had together, we discussed freedom in every aspect, several of those highly intellectually, thanks to how his brain works.

At the end of it, I thought I'd done a great job of not flirting (too much), and had some great insights for my project. We agreed it would be good to meet up again.

We left it another month and then met for dinner. He had invited me to attend an event he was speaking at, and I was keen, but an amazing New Zealand woman entrepreneur was coming to speak at my old school and I was really keen to attend.

So we agreed on a late-ish dinner.

I picked him up from town in my 'freedom mobile', my fast and powerful silver convertible with a licence plate that said 'LVFREE' (Live free).

He didn't look impressed. I later found out that he walked everywhere and didn't own a car.

I immediately noticed how different we were. I was all dressed up from the event, full of socialising women sipping champagne, and he was all calm and grounded and wearing pretty much the same thing as when we first met.

I chatted away; he barely said a word but was a great listener. He was happy with my suggestion of Thai and we happened to be the only two in my fave little restaurant.

That's where the magic happened. Unlike most other

dinners I'd had with men, at this one we immediately did a dissection of the events and what we'd learned. He shared the key concepts of his talk from his slides on his mobile phone, and I shared a summary of what I'd learned too.

We then proceeded to talk about the big picture topics for hours, and continued to do so at an intimate whiskey bar, where we sat very close and I thought we were really into each other.

So imagine my surprise when I dropped him home and he simply said he'd had a lovely night, and goodbye. Not even a kiss on the cheek. What the *heck* had I missed?

I was usually great at the signs, but not with this mysterious man!

The next morning. I get a text message thanking me for the lovely night, and a link to a song, which I thought was the sweetest touch.

We jumped on a call and agreed to go on a date that night.

I trounced him at pool and he beat me at tenpin bowling—our competitive spirits came out and we laughed at each other. We finished the night at a salsa party, where I found out that unlike the perfect man from my list, he didn't like dancing, but he made the effort to pull me for a smoochy dance and that was good enough for me.

We ended the night kissing outside my apartment

building, and were interrupted almost immediately as someone walked out the door at 11 p.m.—which never happens! We felt like two giddy teenagers caught out. It was awesome.

The next day he met my family, by choice, and for the entire next week we barely left my apartment. And for good reason, because exactly a week after our first date I was flying out to London to do my TEDx talk on 'The Surprising Truth About Freedom'. So we made the most of our limited time together.

At the airport, sitting with Mum, I discovered that I'd brought my perfect man list with me, which I'd told Josh about. He was sitting at about 75% and that was good enough for me.

Before I got on the flight, Josh let me know he'd be willing to fly over and meet me in Portugal after my talk, and be a fellow 'digital nomad'. I was blown away at this and agreed with squeals of excitement. I'd met my charming Prince.

The 'Perfect Partner' list really does work. You're not aiming for 'perfect'; you simply want the perfect person for *you*. The person who loves you, warts and all. With no conditions. And you, in turn, can do the same for them. That's where real love begins.

REDEFINE THE RULES OF LOVE AT FIRST SIGHT

Like many women, I was led to believe, from an early age, that a Romeo and Juliet style of love (minus the tragic poisoning and joint death at the end, of course) is truly possible.

If you have a wild imagination, you may even expect that when you're kissing a guy for the first time, music will be playing, fireworks will go off overhead, and everyone around you will start clapping and cheering you on. Then everyone starts dancing, the camera pans out, and you wave with a big cheesy smile as the camera zooms out to capture the whole moment.

Yeah, even as a romantic I know that ain't going to happen. Because true love is about accepting and loving the person you've chosen to be with, not just the moments when they sweep you in their arms, dance you around the floor and then dip you, only to bring you up for a lingering kiss and to utter some loving words in your ear. It's also about loving them in the moments when they're farting, burping, scowling, and being a complete grump.

Yet, if you're like me, you bought into that romanticized, stereotypical version of love to the detriment of actually finding true love.

I pushed Josh away two times, poor guy, before realising what was right in front of me. I could have lost it all, which would have been tragic.

The first was after a beautiful time together in Portugal, where incidentally he witnessed and supported my decision to buy a house after just three weeks there! I recall walking down the beach together in Baleal, on a beautiful morning, holding hands and asking him how he thought we were doing.

He proceeded to tell me how beautiful it was and that he was loving being in love with me.

Then he asked me the same question and I, like an entitled princess, proceeded to tell him why I felt the complete opposite. I simply wasn't prepared or ready for a man who loved me unconditionally, and was so certain about spending his life with me.

I was clinging to my freedom, my independence, my singledom. I convinced myself he wasn't my 'type', which was often tall, muscular, athletic, and fun loving. But deep down I was scared of what this could become and that he might find out I'm not all that he thought I was.

He was disappointed but graceful in hearing me out. To make it worse, I proceeded to pick on things that annoyed me about him, so that I could make it easier on myself to break it off. I somehow managed to focus only on his voice going up at the end of each sentence (one of my biggest bugbears) and couldn't look past it. That was self-sabotage at its worst, and even more so at the expense of hurting him deeply.

When he was due to fly on to an event in Spain, I'd made up my mind he wasn't the one for me. You know, as you do. Finished. Over. Done.

Yet we kept in touch every day through messages. Hardly a day went by when we didn't check in with each other, and if we did happened to miss a day, I felt a little lost or disappointed. I mean really, Nat!

This was a perfect time to tell myself, 'Suck It Up, Princess', and quit being such a bitch and beg for his forgiveness and another chance. Except I was too wrapped up in my own stories.

He began sending me beautiful poems again and we agreed to meet up in the US as originally planned. Once there we were back on, and it was amazing.

I went to events and conferences he was speaking at and he came to mine. I introduced him to dear friends. Then, once again, I had an attack of the doubts and pushed him away.

Patient as ever, he let me have my space.

By absolute chance, we met up in the Dubai airport, both having been in Europe at the same time and we happened to be on the same flight to Brisbane (okay, that's a little Hollywood movie-esque right there), where I was staying a few days before heading home.

We chatted away naturally as if nothing had changed, and in that moment I appreciated what an incredible man he must be, to have me break his heart, not once but twice, and still invite me over to meet his parents in Brisbane and give me a lift to my accommodation.

And that's exactly what happened. His parents were lovely and welcoming, and during our chats with them, he reached over to hold my hand. His capacity to love me knew no bounds and it was about time I respected and honoured him back.

When I got back home I did some thinking and decided to put on my big girl panties and invite him to come and live me with me in my apartment and take this relationship to the next level.

He agreed. The rest is history. A month after he moved in, we were back at New Frontiers, as a couple this time, and while there I looked at a house for sale in the valley the event was held in. A few weeks later I found an amazing house; we put in an offer and when we got back from a trip to Bali we moved in, in April 2017, almost a year after that first cafe meeting.

We are vastly different people and that's what I love. Our values are aligned, and we hold space for each other to be uniquely us.

The key, I've come to realise, is always to communicate openly and with respect and kindness. We can talk through virtually anything, and we share our hopes and dreams together regularly through our LifePilot process we created for that purpose.

This Prince Charming is not the person I ever expected to be with. I mean, heck, he doesn't even like or really play sports, and while he can cook, his idea of a great meal is beans on toast.

Yet these are tiny things compared to the joy, love, laughter, care, intelligence, understanding, loyalty, big picture thinking, cheekiness, and patience he brings to my life.

And he loves me for exactly who I am, and I do my best to do the same back. What's more, I know he and my father would have gotten on so well, like the true gentlemen they are.

If you've been waiting on a fairy-tale romance to happen, and keep being bitterly disappointed, it is likely high time you tell yourself, 'Suck It Up, Princess'.

Then I encourage you to redefine and rewrite the rules of love for what *you* desire, and seek that out.

Talk to couples and your friends in relationships whose love you admire, and ask them what they've found is the key to everlasting, honest, and real love.

THE END. OR IS IT?

So it is that this book, like any good story, has to end.

You've worked on your inner world, learned the art of the Warrior Princess, found your power Princess moves, and stepped into your powerful Queen strength and full-hearted love.

And if I've been a forthright, compassionate, and honest friend to you, you should be in the best possible position to make your life exactly what you wish it to be.

The lesson we repeatedly need to learn in our lifetimes is that the only thing stopping you from living a life you love is you!

In writing this book, as you may have noticed, I've focused on recurring themes around self-love, radical transparency, and showing up in all your beautiful truth.

These qualities, behaviours, and beliefs are very powerful tools we can use to combat our ego, inner critic, imposter syndrome, judging, and meaning-making ways.

This makes way for the true Queens we really are, powerful beyond all measure, perfect in every way, and with no need for magic wands to conjure up our deepest desires and make them a reality.

Quirks, imperfections, moments of doubt, fear, and questionable choices are all part of what makes us deliciously human.

Now, it's up to you to shape your own reality, create your own fairy tale, and do whatever it takes to live in the realm of gratitude and greatness, every single day.

ACKNOWLEDGEMENTS

They say it takes a village to raise a child, and I believe it takes a whole lot more to birth a book.

Most of the time you're grinding it out as the author, letting your imagination take hold, accessing the deepest recesses of your brain, rekindling old stories for better or worse, learning every time you write how little you truly know.

Then there's the team of supporters around you, near and far, rooting for you, bringing you energy, inspiration, and encouragement when you need it most.

If you're reading this book then I damn well hope you know who you are.

Special mentions go to my parents, Peter and Gina—one looking down on me from above who inspired in me the love of the English language and writing from an early age, and one here on earth who inspired me by bringing me into this world, and writing and publishing her own memoirs at age 78, in the same month I finished this book.

To my sister, Deb, for sharing endless fun hours as young girls, dreaming up reality stories for our Barbie dolls and our Smurf and Lego collections. To this day I reckon that is where our most creative moments began!

To my Prince Charming, my Lumber Josh. Words can do you no justice, so I blow you a kiss filled with love and tenderness for making our life together so much richer in every way. Your help in molding the ideas in this book into some kind of logical structure was totally appreciated on those late night and early morning conversations.

To Kara Northcott, for taking the plunge in supporting me and becoming the first $10K Club Queen in style. To Matthew Monaghan, for your belief in and support of me, and the steady supply of delicious homemade almond milk. To Omar and Nicole Zenholm, for your generous support of this book and for being on the entrepreneurial journey with me, and to Tash Corbin, you're a kindred spirit in all things heart-centered business.

To my fellow 'Write the Damn Book' authors and supporters on this epic journey: Abby Connick, Alina Siegfried, Amber Hawley, Claudia Gross, Donna Ghaemaghamy, Elise Darma, Francis Ayley, Honor Mathieson, Jen Campbell, Jo Bendle, Michael Burns, Michelle Prior, Natalie Cutler-Welsh, Nicole Marcione, Rachel Ann Harding, Sarah Potter, Suzy Rock-Evans, and Terry Neithercut. We did it!

To Kate Peterson, Kim Morrison, Lorraine Hamilton, Miranda Clayton, Osmaan Sharif, Rivka Hodgkinson, Roxanne Reid, Ruby McGill, and Tracey Northcott, so much gratitude for your early support in pre-ordering this book when it was just an idea.

The same goes to you: Saeema Salim, Allison A. Bailes III, Cathy Goddard, Jesse Krieger, Louise Vallack, Nancy Zevely, Susanne Östman, Tia Lloyd and Timothy McElroy, Alicia Michelle, Allyson Machate, Andrea Whitwam, Angela Clancy, Ashley Grant, Ava Callaway, Barbara Wood, Bronwyn Jackson, Brooklin Kennedy, Caelan Huntress, Carin Newbould, Casey Lynch, Cathy Goddard, Claire Alderton, Claire Dinsmore, David Dreyfus, Denise Monahan, Elizabeth Saunders, Fiona Pullen, Fiona Buchet, Heather Scott, Heidi Vial, Hendrik Kuiper, Jennifer Lachs, Jennifer Heuett, Jess Haney, Jill Calogaras, Julia Capon, Kari Lloyd Kat Lintott, Katharine Transue , Kathryn Curzon, Katie Clarke, Kim McCormick, Kirsty Nielsen, Lee Constantine, Lorraine Minister, Melissa Ratti, Michelle Falzon, Michelle Mazur, Olie Body, Rebecca Jarus, Sarah Mikutel, Sarah Weaver, Shelly Brown, Syliva van de Logt, T N Thomas, Tara Ciecko, Tathra Street, Teresa Adams, and Zena Bruges and Trafton Crandall. I truly thank you all!

To all my fellow Warrior Princesses, you have all the power you need within you.

ABOUT THE AUTHOR

NATALIE SISSON is a New Zealand entrepreneur, author, speaker, host of the 'Untapped' podcast, and eternal optimist.

After ditching a successful corporate career and co-founding a technology company, Natalie decided to monetise her humble, six-month-old blog, The Suitcase Entrepreneur, into a multiple-six-figure online education platform back in 2010.

In her efforts to continuously innovate, Natalie, the OG of digital nomads, has since turned that content and knowledge into eight different revenue streams including digital products, courses, workshops, international retreats, and coaching.

These days, she's passionate about helping others leverage their unique set of skills, knowledge, and experience to earn a living and make an impact from anywhere, simply by being them.

Natalie believes that everyone has their own unique potential and she's here to show you how to tap into it, get paid to be you and create a purpose-driven life and business.

As a leading learner, teacher, advisor and performance coach, she works with you to combine your passions, skills and expertise and turn them into profitable products and offerings that make an impact on others.

She does this through her online resources, courses, membership, and podcast.

Natalie's a two-time Amazon No #1 bestselling author, a sought-after speaker, and named as one of Huffington Post's 50 Must-Follow Women Entrepreneurs in 2017.

She's a contributor to Thrive, Forbes, and Lifehack, and has featured on many other publications and media outlets including 60 Minutes, Yahoo Finance, Huffington Post, Guardian, Daily Mail, Sydney Herald, Mashable, and more.

Born in Wellington, New Zealand, she returned home from a decade of world travels in 2017 and lives a lifestyle she loves with her partner, Josh, and their two gorgeous white German Shepherds on their beautiful rural property.

LETTER OF LOVE TO MY READERS

I so appreciate you reading my book *Suck It Up, Princess.*

Do you know what I appreciate even more? You acting on what you've read and stepping into your truly powerful Princess panties!

Even better is telling me, in an Amazon(ian) Princess review, how this book made you feel, act, or believe. The more stars the better, thank you!

If you want to learn how to make the income you deserve and the impact you desire, simply by being you, come on over to nataliesisson.com

If you want to keep on tapping into your full potential and learning with me and through my inspirational guests, then listen into my weekly Untapped podcast at nataliesisson.com/podcast.

If you're intrigued about my $10K Club, want to grow your business to six figures and beyond, while making a ripple effect in others' lives, come join us women-inspiring-women at nataliesisson.com/10K.

If you want to turn your dreams into reality, one day at a time, checkout LifePilot.co.

If you want to finally launch your damn online coure and get paid to teach others what you know, then download my free starter kit at nataliesisson.com/coursekit

If you want to check out my other number one bestselling books, head to nataliesisson.com/books for more details on where to buy *The Suitcase Entrepreneur* and *The Freedom Plan*.

CPSIA information can be obtained
at www.ICGtesting.com
Printed in the USA
LVHW051114120621
690063LV00009B/969